History's Daughter

The Life of Clara Endicott Sears
Founder of Fruitlands Museums

Cynthia H. Barton

Fruitlands Museums
Harvard, Massachusetts

History's Daughter
The Life of Clara Endicott Sears
Founder of Fruitlands Museums
by Cynthia H. Barton

Copyright © 1988
Fruitlands Museums, Inc.
Harvard, Massachusetts

Fruitlands Museums, Inc. Publication Number 3
International Standard Book Number: 0-941632-02-4
Library of Congress Catalogue Card Number: 88-082411
Printed in the United States of America by
Arcata Graphics, Braintree, Massachusetts

Clara Endicott Sears, 1863-1960

Contents

Illustrations

(following page 64)

(All illustrations are from the Fruitlands collections.)

WINTHROP AND SEARS FAMILIES

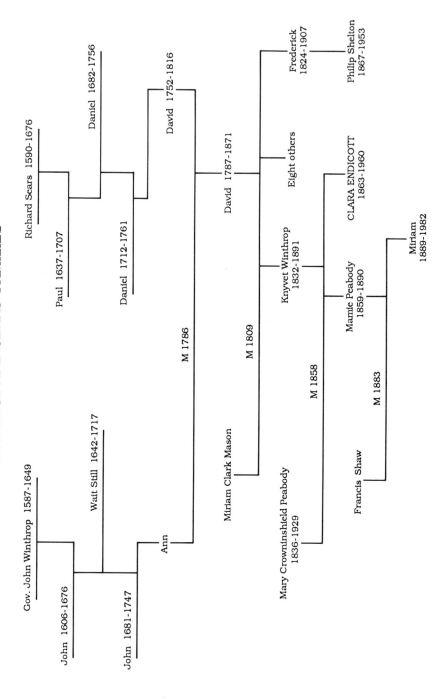

ENDICOTT AND PEABODY FAMILIES

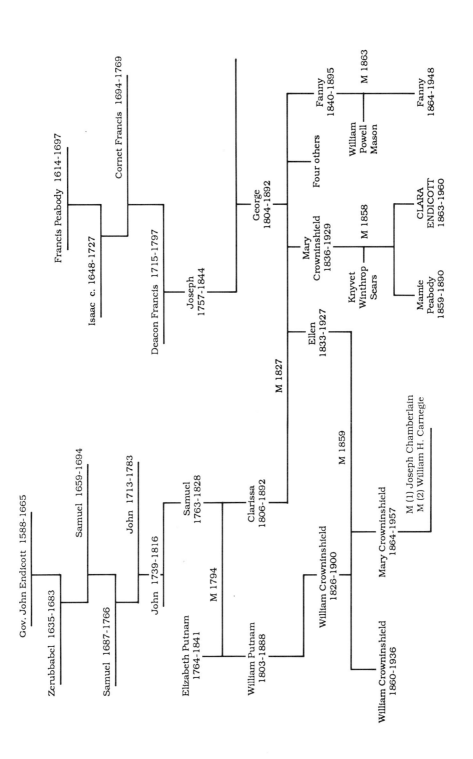

Introduction

Clara Endicott Sears was a Boston Brahmin who preferred intellectual to social pursuits, a strong-willed woman of inherited wealth whose Victorian upbringing made her wary of exchanging filial duty for marital obedience. She preferred not to marry but, at age twenty-eight, insisted on a self-imposed obligation as companion to her widowed mother. Born in 1863, Miss Sears lived well into her ninety-seventh year, gratefully aware of the family heritage of longevity, for it was not until her fiftieth year that she found her professional niche.

As she entered middle age, she became increasingly frustrated that no tangible evidence of her intellectual interests could possibly emerge from a routine of social work and benefits, luncheons and teas. In 1910, she compromised with her sense of duty and established her own summer household in Harvard, Massachusetts, a fortunate change that led ultimately to her career as an author and preservationist.

Her new home, the Pergolas, overlooked Fruitlands, the site of Bronson Alcott's unsuccessful 1843 experiment in communal living. In restoring the farmhouse and in her research for *Bronson Alcott's Fruitlands*, Miss Sears formed friendships with Alcott heirs as well as with local Shakers whose predecessors had carried on lively philosophical debates with Alcott and Charles Lane. The Shakers entrusted their precious journals to Miss Sears, and in her growing empathy with them she became imbued with much of their mysticism, though she balanced it with a firm and forthright New England practicality.

Descended from the Massachusetts Bay Colony's first two colonial governors, John Endicott and John Winthrop, she was intrigued early on by the fact that from the Pergolas she could see Mt. Wachusett where, in the 1670's, King Philip, Chief Metacom, had gathered together Algonquin chiefs in a futile effort to form a confederation against encroaching English settlers. Her volume, *The Great Powwow*, demonstrates a unique understanding of the Indian cause and of King Philip who was, as she put it, one of America's first patriots.

Though her own is a success story, it was of failed utopias that Miss Sears wrote, and it was in their memory that she established several museums on the grounds of her Harvard estate. At her death, in 1960, she left as her legacy the Fruitlands Museums, Inc., fourteen books, and the example of personal achievement brought about solely by her own efforts in an era when such determination in a woman was the exception rather than the rule.

CHAPTER 1

Naumkeag

All honor, then, to the memory of
John Endicott, and may he never
want for an illustrious descendant.

Hon. Robert C. Winthrop, 1878,
250th celebration of the landing
of Governor Endicott

Thanksgiving dinner at the home of George and Clarissa Peabody of Salem, Massachusetts, was an elaborate affair. Extra staff was hired, and members of the extended family began to arrive by mid-afternoon for a four o'clock meal. The men wore swallow-tail coats and white cravats; the women were resplendent in long gowns of velvet or satin and lace. In November of 1867, the Peabodys' three-year-old granddaughters, Clara Sears and Mary Endicott, were called upon to perform a strange holiday custom called walking the table. The object was to traverse the length of the well-laden board without succumbing to the temptations of sweetmeats, fruits, and candies along the way. Each was dressed in white muslin with a colored sash and matching ankle ties, and each wore coral beads about her neck. Their grandfather shouted "Go!" and "two little mites" set forth from opposite ends, finding their way through the goodies. Meeting midway,

1

they were sorely tempted by candy roosters beckoning from the cut glass saucers of a silver epergne, but they resisted temptation and proceeded on to exclamations of "the little darlings" and "weren't they wise though!" Mary was decorously lifted from her end of the table, but the applause went to Clara's "small bedazzled head," and in a burst of exuberance she leaped onto her grandmother's lap, nearly toppling them both onto the floor.

Clara Endicott Sears and her cousin Mary Endicott were close friends throughout their entire lives. It was due to the typical Endicott stubbornness of Aunt Eliza Endicott Perry that Mary survived at birth, for she was pronounced stillborn by the attending physicians. Aunt Perry, refusing to accept the verdict, wrapped the infant in blankets, built a fire in the nursery, and breathed into the newborn's mouth until she at last felt the stir of a heartbeat. It was fortunate for her cousin that Mary's life was thus saved, for Mary became one of the few people in whom the reticent Clara was able to confide.

In 1956, when both were in their nineties, Mary helped Clara decide upon childhood episodes to include in her *Early Personal Reminiscences*, a small volume for friends and relatives that set forth her Salem memories with great warmth. They easily agreed on their earliest shared memory, walking the table, and then went on to select favorites from their later childhood. Clara had an older sister, Mamie, and Mary had an older brother, William. The four were "a jolly quartet." The Endicotts lived on Essex Street, not far from the Peabody mansion on Washington Square. The Sears girls were brought up on Beacon Street, Boston, but loved to visit Salem and did so at every possible opportunity.

Clara and Mamie were the daughters of socially prominent Victorian parents, Knyvet and Mary Sears. In Boston the girls saw little of them; at their grandparents' home in Salem the elders were more accessible, putting aside the demands of society for summer picnics, winter sleigh rides, and the gaiety of large family gatherings at Thanksgiving and Christmas.

2

Children were part of the festivities at Washington Square. "The jolly quartet" entertained the grown-ups with dress-up improvisations after Thanksgiving dinners. Antique gowns and cloaks awaited them in well-filled attic trunks, from which the elder two selected the choicest garments for themselves. One year Mamie appeared as a Gainsborough portrait in pale blue brocade and a leghorn hat, while William became a young George Washington in white wig, three-cornered hat, buckle shoes, and black satin knee breeches. Mary and Clara were "a rag tag pair" in ill-fitting satins and laces and looked "a queer sight." Once again the adults were lavish with praise, filling the children's ears with "Aren't they cute" and "What a lovely picture." As a woman of ninety-two, writing her reminiscences, Clara Sears recalled the praise and felt such approbation to have been an integral part of her childhood experiences. Early on, she became finely tuned to the perfection expected of her. As an adult she expected it of herself, still requiring praise although she had become confidently independent in her actions, often to the point of an off-putting abruptness.

Self-confidence was a natural result of the approval Clara earned while growing up, as well as of the wealth to which she was born and the respect accorded her family. Her heritage had not a little to do with the security of her position. Through the marriage of her parents, Knyvet Winthrop Sears and Mary Peabody, she was descended from two early governors of the Massachusetts Bay Colony, John Endicott on her mother's side and John Winthrop on her father's. In 1628, Governor Endicott was sent to Salem by the London Plantation. His charge was to salvage this struggling fishing settlement, which was then called Naumkeag. One of Clara's favorite family stories included picturesque details about his arrival on the ship *Abigail*. Since the tide was at its lowest, the new governor was borne to shore on the shoulders of three men who rolled up their pantaloons and waded into the water for the purpose. Visual imagery captured Clara's imagination early on.

In the autumn of 1878, when Clara was an impressionable fourteen years of age, the town of Salem celebrated the 250th anniversary of John Endicott's landing. As a direct descendant, much was made of Clara, and she awoke eagerly to the bright and cloudless September day. Dean Stanley of Westminster Abbey, a featured speaker, was impressed that even in England few towns could boast of so many families which had lived in one place for so many generations. He singled out the Peabodys for a special visit, calling on them with the Reverend Phillips Brooks, who was staying with the Endicotts during the festivities. Clara's uncle, Judge William C. Endicott, gave the commemorative address to the general public, and then two hundred invited guests sat down to luncheon in Hamilton Hall, the traditional meeting place for Salem's social events. On the cover of the printed menu was a likeness of Governor Endicott and a facsimile of his signature. The original portrait, taken from life, was hanging in the home of the Endicotts, where it had long been a familiar sight to Clara. The luncheon address by the Honorable Robert Winthrop further reinforced her pride in being descended from both governors, for he devoted much of his talk to the friendship between Endicott and Winthrop. She and Mamie were the only two in the hall who were distinguished by such a combined and prestigious ancestry.

Knyvet Winthrop Sears was the grandson of Ann Winthrop and David Sears of Boston, whose great wealth was acquired through the China trade. Mary Crowninshield Peabody was the daughter of Clarissa Endicott and George Peabody, whose fortune was similarly acquired. Even as a girl, Clara emulated the Puritan work ethic, boasting that her hands were never idle. By adulthood, the need to fill her time constructively was almost compulsive. Remembering her youth, she included in *Early Personal Reminiscences* a photograph of a silk-lined sewing basket with lace trimmings, which she had made at the age of seven. By the age of ten she had replaced needlework with intellectual pursuits, however, reading voraciously under the guidance of her grandmother, Clarissa Peabody, and probably trying her hand at poetry at the instigation of George Peabody.

Clara's colonial ancestors believed that worldly success was exclusively the reflection of the Lord's satisfaction with one's hard work and piety. As an adult, she was known to be just but not generous with her money. Her life was exemplified by thrift, a sense of duty, hard work, and a strong religious faith. She was a devout Episcopalian but felt understanding toward any religion truly held. She was thus much more tolerant than her ancestors, who had come to America in order to worship as they pleased but, in so doing, persecuted those who took open exception to Puritanism. Initially, Governors Endicott and Winthrop were not Separatists as were the Plymouth Pilgrims, but they were nonconformists, objecting to many of the ceremonies of the Church of England. When colonists John and Samuel Browne insisted on continuing the use of the Book of Common Prayer, Governor Endicott summarily banished them to England as "unfit persons" whose conduct would lead to schism and anarchy.

The colonists were beset by severe physical privations as well as spiritual controversy. If the settlement were to survive, a strong hand was needed. Though the new church imposed no restrictions on church membership in respect to race or class, only those who agreed with its tenets were admitted to membership, and only church members held the franchise. The very existence of the colony was felt to depend upon suppressing, punishing, or banishing those who openly expressed beliefs that threatened to subvert either church or state. This attitude was expressed by the General Court, Massachusetts Bay's governing body, in a report to the Royal Commissioners which stated that "subjection to ecclesiastical discipline was necessary for the well being of any Christian society."

In his zeal, Governor Endicott overstepped his bounds in September of 1634, when he publicly defaced the royal ensign of King Charles I with a sword familiar to Clara, for it had been passed down through the generations and was in the possession of Cousin Mary Endicott's father. John Endicott willfully slashed the cross from the flag "because it represented to him both ecclesiastical and monarchical superstition." So that England might not take offense as the result of such a treasonable act, Endicott was "disabled for one year from bearing any public office, declining any heavier sentence because they [The General Court] were persuaded he did it out of tenderness of conscience, and not of any evil intent."

This brash manner persevered through generations of Endicotts and was typified by Clara's great-great-great grandmother, Elizabeth Endicott, who lived to the age of ninety-one and never hesitated to say what she thought. She had impatient words for Colonel Timothy Pickering on the day of the battle of Bunker Hill. As he halted his company briefly near the Endicott farm, she expressed her disapproval of the delay. "Why on earth don't you march; don't you hear the guns at Charlestown?" Such were the models set before young Endicotts of Salem.

When, as a single woman fifty years of age, Clara Endicott Sears finally found the way to establish a household of her own, she ordered her servants in much the same terse way as Elizabeth Endicott had ordered Pickering's army. She required adherence to her expectations and exactitude regarding schedules. Those without high personal standards need not apply, nor would they last long if inadvertently hired. She was neither unkind nor unfair, but her Puritan-straight posture and manner set her apart. White-haired for more than half of her long life and active well into her nineties, she was a small feminine figure whose clothing of softly draped fabrics contrasted with her stern manner. With her mother, she was chauffeured about the countryside near the summer residence which represented her independence - Miss Sears, slight of build; Mrs. Sears, Peabodyplump.   The inseparable pair raised gloved hands, queen-like, and nodded wide brimmed hats in unison, inspiring awe in children by the roadside.   Even in her home, Miss Sears wore her hat, giving the impression that she was about to leave and that the casual caller would not be long welcome.   Such austerity of bearing was inherent in her background and personality but essential, as well, for the protection of her creativity.   She had no patience with trifles; it was essential that her household run smoothly and that she have ample time for her work of research, writing, collecting, and historic restoration.

Clara Endicott Sears gave luncheons in preference to dinner parties so as to have her evenings free for writing.   Her guest lists reflected her desire to share her interests with others similarly wellborn and intellectually inclined.   She was unabashedly class conscious, and social bounds were not to be crossed.   Her prejudices were born of wealth and position, however, and she was fair according to her lights.   By the 1930s, in her eighth decade, when she was at last a recognized author and preservationist, she invited two prominent Indians to be honored guests and sacred performers at the opening of her Indian museum.   David Buffalo Bear was a Chief of the Sioux, and Wo Peen was an artist from the Ildefonso Pueblo.   Since Miss Sears observed prescribed social roles, and one did not dine with one's chauffeur, a problem arose. She tactfully saw to it that Chief Buffalo Bear's driver took his luncheon "with the chauffeur group."   On the other hand, Wo Peen's patron, Mr. Cushman, who always drove him, "couldn't be relegated to David's chauffeur's group" as he had "three Mayflower lines."

Despite the fact that Miss Sears' ancestor, Governor John Endicott, had been unyielding and quick to anger, he set a precedent for fairness to Native Americans which Clara Sears pursued in her turn.   In 1660, the General Court approved a unique deed of land from the Indians to John Endicott, Jr., "considering the many kindnesses that were shewne to the Indians by our honored Governour in the infancy of these plantations."   Almost three hundred years later, Clara Endicott Sears wrote *The Great Pow-wow*, which exhibited an unusual understanding of the Indian Confederation formed by Chief Metacom to oust white intruders during what became known as King Philip's War. She built a sympathetic case for the fact that Metacom, a man of high birth and exceptional intelligence, was a true patriot in behalf of a losing cause.

It is on her work as the historian of such lost utopias that Miss Sears' reputation rests. Her research was inspired by the auspicious location of her summer home near the scene of several early communal societies; and her identification with Bay State history was fostered by an abundance of ancestral anecdotes. Peabodys took part in the American Revolution as did Endicotts. Although Clara's great-grandfather Joseph Peabody was but a lad at the time and too young to enroll in the militia officially, he volunteered his services without enrollment and headed off to join the Minutemen at Lexington and Concord. By the time the company arrived the battle was over, but he later signed as a sailor on a succession of privateers, including the *Bunker Hill, Pilgrim,* and *Ranger.* This taste of the sea led to a lucrative career as a shipbuilder and merchant, and so successful was he that toward the end of his life he was one of the most wealthy men of his time. It was said that he paid annual taxes of $200,000, and his biographer claimed "his reputation was such that his credit was held equal to the government's."

For a while, Joseph Peabody employed William Putnam Endicott, Clarissa Endicott Peabody's brother, in his counting house. Though Clara's recollection of her great-uncle had become somewhat romanticized by the time she wrote *Early Personal Reminiscences,* her impressions were not dimmed by time.

If ever there was a perfect example in looks of our Puritan ancestors, here was one of them. I can see him now in memory solemnly walking up Essex Street, enveloped in a long, voluminous black cloak reaching below the knees, beneath which was an even longer black coat. He wore his hair long enough to curl up at the ends halfway to his shoulders. All this was topped off by a black hat with a wide brim that concealed his face. All one could see was two penetrating eyes and a very long Puritan upper lip. I used to be afraid of him when I was a child. I didn't believe he could smile, but I have been told by those who knew, that he was a kindly man, but frightened to death of women.

There was a succession of William Endicotts, and this first one was the grandfather of Clara's cousin, William. According to Cousin William, William P. Endicott owed much in his demeanor to stern paternal discipline. His dignified adult gait was the result of a drastic lesson learned when a young boy. He had often been told, while taking Sunday strolls about Salem with his father, to turn out his toes. Exasperated by the boy's inattention to this important detail, his father terminated one outing with a curt "I won't walk with a boy who does not turn out his toes!"

In his Endicott memoir, Cousin William went on to relate that even as an adult, there was no respite for William P. Endicott.

> Later in life [he] had been away from Salem some two years on a voyage to the East, and as Captain of the ship he brought her into Salem harbor on a wild winter night in January, in the midst of a snow storm and gale. Landing at the wharf he walked home and reached his father's house long after midnight. In trying to arouse the household, a window over the side door was opened and a voice said, "Who's there?" "William," was the reply. "You ought to be ashamed to bring a ship into Salem harbor on a night like this," said his father. The window was slammed down and the son went back to his ship. This was advice which the son never forgot and which he always said was of help to him in after voyages.

William P. Endicott was not only a seafaring man but also an avid horticulturist and a classical scholar, a gentleman who retired early to a New Hampshire farm in order to follow his pastimes in comfortable seclusion. His sister, Clarissa Endicott Peabody, was much more sociable than he although she did choose to visit with friends and family in her own home in preference to going to theirs. She, too, loved her garden and shared his regard for literature. It was unusual for girls of the early 1800s to receive academic instruction outside of the home, but the Endicotts valued knowledge. A receipt dated November 1, 1813, indicated payment by Samuel Endicott to B & H King for the tuition of his daughter from April 1 to October 1. Instruction was four dollars and fuel two. Clarissa's personal regard for learning carried her far beyond the simple education allowed to girls of her day. She read voraciously all her life, retained what she learned, and shared her knowledge and enthusiasm first with her own large family and then with her grandchildren.

Clara Endicott Sears was Clarissa's namesake, having been born on December 16, 1863, the anniversary of her grandmother's birth, and there was always a very close bond between them. Clarissa lived for her family and as she rarely went neighboring, she was always available during Clara's visits to Salem. In Boston, on the other hand, Clara was accustomed to having her mother summon their carriage almost daily in order to pursue her social rounds.

Clarissa Peabody combined warmth and understanding with constant intellectual stimulation and high personal standards. Clara early adopted her grandmother's daily motto, "Give out something from within," and she never forgot her admonition to keep a furnished mind. Clarissa maintained that reading aloud from the works of famous authors, even to very young children, would engender in them a love of literature even if little was actually understood at the time. She was right. Some of Clara's fondest memories were of Christmas and New Year's Eves spent with her cousins, gathered around their grandmother's rocking chair in her little parlor, listening to her read from Dickens and recite poetry. Tennyson's "Ring out, wild bells, to the wild sky," she recalled, not only charged the atmosphere with "the spirit of romance and joyous anticipation of the coming year, but there was a spiritual as well as a literary vibration...that made a deep impression upon all of us."

Clarissa Peabody was also eminently practical, a fact that Clara attributed to her being an Endicott. Clara, too, looked matters squarely in the face and acted accordingly, but a complementary influence worked upon her through her grandfather. He had much of the dreamer about him, and Clara never forgot the quiet inspiration of childhood hours spent with George Peabody, who composed music and poetry, played the violin, and painted in oils. He had a little studio at the top of his Washington Square mansion, a haven into which he could escape from noisy family gatherings below. From a very early age, Clara was one of the few invited to this private sanctuary. She was fully aware of the privilege thus extended to her, and during these visits she learned to understand and value artistic creation.

George Peabody composed on an Amati violin, and Clara used to listen in awe as melodies came floating down from the upper story. She felt at such times that a sense of mystery pervaded the atmosphere. George teased Clarissa about reading the classics to toddling grandchildren, and she in turn questioned him as to what possible fascination there could be for Clara in the little room at the top of the house. Clara remembered hearing her say, "Lor, whatever does that child want to go up there for?" But go she did, thus placing more and more distance between her tastes and those of the socialite world which was her Boston birthright.

Clara described her enthusiasm in *Early Personal Reminiscences.*

> My grandfather for some reason seemed to sense the fact that, little child that I was, I had it in me to have some understanding of the things that interested him, and every now and then he would ask me to go up there, saying that he had something to show me. To say that I clambered up that little narrow flight of stairs in a fever of anticipation and

ran headlong into the room does not express it. It was a blaze of sunshine there, and two robins and a catbird were flying about, evidently feeling very much at home.

"They arrived on date this morning," my grandfather explained. "In what clime they have been wintering we cannot tell, but this was their date for returning. I opened the window wide and sure enough in they came and sat on my knee, and I gave them their breakfast. I wanted you to see them and to learn that man is not the only creature to whom God has given intelligence; he has given it to the birds as well."

Sometimes I would linger a long time in that room, and one time he took me to the window. Day was coming to its close and the sky was still radiant with rays from the setting sun. "Remember, little Clara," he said, "you will never see a sky like that again. Every sky is different. The Almighty creates everything new."

It is easy to understand why Clara Endicott Sears had a more sober nature than that of Boston's society belles. A likeness of her at age seven, painted by George Southward, showed her in a white dress with a tucked front, a large plaid sash, and matching shoulder ribbons. A great abundance of wavy hair was pulled back from her face and held with a band; but her eyes were the striking feature of the portrait. They were dark and pensive, the same doleful eyes of subsequent portraits and photographs, which in adolescence lent her an air of wistfulness but in childhood suggested a premature and startling profundity. She was a serious child just as she was a serious adult.

CHAPTER 2

The City on the Hill

*Therefore lett us choose life, that wee
and our Seede, may live; by obeyeing his
voyce, and cleaveing to him, for hee is
our life, and our prosperity.*

Governor John Winthrop
"A Modell of Christian Charity"

Clara's father, Knyvet Winthrop Sears, met her mother, Mary Crowninshield Peabody, through Mary's brother, who was Knyvet's Harvard College friend and companion. Most of the Peabody clan referred to Mary as Molly, and during their courtship Knyvet called her his "little broccoli sprout." Engagements were formalized in the large drawing room of the Peabodys' Washington Square home. Traditionally, everyone knew what was afoot but pretended ignorance, and it wasn't until Clarissa tinkled a bell and servants brought in cake, hot buttered toast, and homemade brandy wine that suppressed excitement was released by the anticipated announcement. Clara herself witnessed such a scene when her aunt, Sarah Endicott, became engaged to George Dexter. She had been playing Indians in the library adjoining the drawing room when she realized that the grown-ups were up to something special. Peeking around the portiere that hung over

13

the door, she watched as Matthew Moran, the butler, and Julia, the housemaid, were invited to join the family in toasts to the newly engaged couple. Interrupted in her game of Indians, Clara resisted with great difficulty the impulse to shoot them all with her make-believe arrows. She had not yet become the sentimentalist of later years.

It was the custom for the betrothed of Salem to stroll in the cemetery, and the Peabody girls did not think it peculiar. Knyvet Sears did, however, as Clara well knew from a family anecdote. Soon after their engagement Knyvet came from Boston for a four o'clock dinner with the Peabodys. Afterward, Molly suggested a walk and they had not gone far before he asked where they were going. "To the cemetery of course," was her reply. "To the cemetery!" Knyvet shouted. "What in the name of all the saints and the prophets are *we* doing in a cemetery?" As the alternative path led to Gallows Hill where the witches had been hanged, he chose the cemetery as perhaps "the more cheerful of the two."

Clara was a child of the Victorian age, born in 1863, when a respectful distance was maintained between generations. She was attended largely by nursemaids and observed her parents' comings and goings with a certain amount of objectivity. In *Early Personal Reminiscences* she compared her mother with aunts who had also arrived for Thanksgiving dinner at the Peabodys. "Smaller than the others, but dainty to a degree, with coal black hair and flashing dark eyes and a skin as white as the camellia she wore in her hair. I remember her dress was a very pale lavender satin, and I swelled with pride when I saw her with my father by her side." Truly proud of her parents, Clara was also pleased that their appearance measured up to that of the others.

After Thanksgiving dinners, Mrs. Sears always played the piano for dancing in the large drawing room. Music was an interest she shared with her daughters, and Clara's older sister Mamie probably spelled her now and then, for children participated in the gaieties at Washington Square. Clara's instrument was the violin, attempted none too successfully under the influence of

George Peabody. Neither she nor her grandfather fiddled for Thanksgiving dancing although a Virginia reel usually ended the evening. The furniture of the large drawing room was moved aside, of course, and the elaborate decor seems not to have inhibited the dancers. The room showed the French influence of its decorator, Lamonier, whom George Peabody had engaged for the job while he was in Paris in the 1820s. The walls as well as the upholstered furniture were covered in beige brocade, figured with royal blue, and a frieze around the top of the room depicted a classical boar hunt. A gilt ormolu clock and two large branching candelabra, also of gilt, stood upon the mantel, in front of a very large gilt framed mirror. The whole was lit by a huge gilt chandelier and matching wall sconces. The suppers served in this room by the caterer, Cassell, were correspondingly elaborate. To conclude the holiday festivities, Endicotts and Peabodys feasted on scalloped oysters, chicken salad, and ice cream, with champagne, brandy, or cordial for the adults.

It was customary for members of these two families to spend months at a time abroad. They felt an affinity for the French, especially after General Lafayette's 1824 visit to Salem, where a ball was held in his honor at Hamilton Hall. George Peabody, then a young man, had quite a lengthy conversation with this French marquis who had given his help to George Washington during our Revolution. When Peabody sailed for France on mercantile matters not long after, he was invited to a banquet given by Lafayette. Upon learning that the young American was a musician, the Marquis insisted that he teach the orchestra to play "Yankee Doodle." "But, Monsieur Marquis," he exclaimed, "I have not got the music with me; I could not possibly give you any idea how it should go." Lafayette said, "Oh, never mind that, Monsieur Peabody; whistle it to the orchestra, and I'll wager they will play it." The resulting cacaphony sounded more like "Turkey in the Straw" than "Yankee Doodle". Clara loved this anecdote for its own sake, but it also added not a little to her respect for her family and hence for herself.

French was the second tongue of cultivated Bostonians and Salemites. Clara and Mamie were fluent in the language, thanks as much to instruction by their parents as to year-long trips abroad. Their father was something of a French scholar, and the Sears family lived in Europe, largely in France, from August of 1872 to November of 1873. They also spent the year 1877 in foreign travel. Although Clara received some formal schooling at the establishments of the Misses Sanger and Foote on Boston's Beacon Hill, her true education took place abroad. Mrs. Sears, through reading and her own travel, had become extremely knowledgeable. It was she who taught Mamie and Clara about the past of all the places they visited; it was she who kindled in Clara an interest in historical events beyond those involving her own family. Since the girls' instruction was dependent upon their mutual presence at places of interest, they saw much more of their mother in Europe than at home and regarded their outings as special treats.

Back in Boston, Mrs. Sears' busy social schedule, her involvement with the Chilton Club, and her active role in the charities of Emmanuel Church precluded any great intimacy with the girls. They were even less close to their father, although his study of photography in the Paris studio of Gustav Legray had fostered in Clara a similar interest. Even as an adolescent she was searching for an appropriate way in which to express her creativity. She sensed that she had no genius for music or art. Photography was only a hobby. She had no premonition that she would eventually forge a career out of her appreciation for history. One constant in her life, however, was her insistence upon doing things herself and in her own way. Neither gentility nor gender could dissuade her from doing all her photographic developing and printing herself. In fact, she became quite proficient and, in 1890, received the Photography Association of America's silver medal for landscape subjects.

According to the annals of Harvard's class of 1852, Knyvet Winthrop Sears was "a typical gentleman of an age now passed, with the cultivated tastes of a man of leisure." His consuming interest was in matters equestrian. Horses, of course, were a necessity during Clara's childhood. Cast iron watering troughs abounded, and the ringing of blacksmiths' hammers upon anvils was a common sound. There were so many private stables on Beacon Hill's lower Chestnut Street that it acquired the nickname Horsechestnut. Public trolleys jingled along their routes, marked by identifying colors and drawn upon rails by paired horses. Conductors knew their passengers by name and stopped upon request, anywhere along the line, to pick up or discharge them, sometimes tarrying at a stop to await a regular who was a bit behindtimes.

Though Knyvet Sears was as concerned as the next man about the quality of his carriage horses, his passion was for racing his thoroughbred trotters. In the Boston of Clara's childhood, the road to Longwood and Brookline was clear for such sport during the afternoon hours. In the mornings, large herds of steers could be encountered as they were driven on their way to the Brighton abattoir, but afternoons were sufficiently clear for racing. The races began on Boston's old Mill Dam which still separated the Charles River from the unfilled portion of the Back Bay. These contests, as Clara remembered them, "revealed the sporting spirit hidden under the waistcoats of Boston gentlemen."

Whereas Clara's recollections of Salem events usually revealed a close intimacy with her Peabody grandfather, the manner in which she recounted her father's trotting race was that of a detached observer. His interests, except for photography, were not hers. Her narrative of the event was impersonal.

A policeman was procured to give the signal for the start and off they went, seemingly quiet and sedate gentlemen until they were seated behind their trotters, then the lids were lifted, and the shouts that came from them were appalling, shouting at their horses, urging them on, shouting at

17

their companions for a moment become rivals, or at one who was foolish enough to cross their path. Such a transformation in them seemed unbelievable. Dr. Sprague, habitually a mild and most kindly man, made the echoes ring with his shouts, but all admitted that nothing had ever been heard equal to Mr. John Shepard. His language was such as to terrify the most hardened jockey. He could be heard from a distance bellowing vociferously his imprecations that scattered the unwary from right to left.

When Knyvet Sears' father, David Sears the Younger, was a boy, cows were still grazed on Boston Common. Boston was a hilly peninsula connected to the mainland at Roxbury by a narrow neck of land. The view from the top of Beacon Hill was of water, be it deep harbor, tidal basins, or vast marshes. There was no Charles Street, no Public Garden, none of today's alphabetically ordered streets from Arlington to Hereford. Knyvet Winthrop Sears was among the first to live on the extension of Beacon Street created when land was reclaimed from the Back Bay to form Boston's fashionable new residential area.

Clara's father's family was as wealthy and prominent as her mother's, and as distinguished in its colonial forebears. In 1630, when John Winthrop arrived in Salem with the royal charter and seals, John Endicott, who had been governing the initial settlement, relinquished his post and the seat of government was removed to Boston. With the exception of Endicott's one year "punishment," these two men served the rest of their lives in public office, and each died while holding the position of governor.

Clara's other ancestors arrived in the New World equally early. Francis Paybody, or Pabodie, arrived in Ipswich in 1636; Richard Seeres, or Sares, known as Richard the Pilgrim by his descendants, was listed on the tax rolls of Plymouth Colony in 1633. He took "the oath of Fidellyte" in 1653 and became juryman, constable, and representative to the General Court. In 1763, his great-great-grandson, David Sears the Elder, moved to Boston and, like Joseph Peabody, made a fortune in the East India and China trades. Through his later association with the

18

First Bank of the United States he acquired the islands at the mouth of the Penobscot River in what was then the District of Maine, and the town of Searsport was named in his honor.

David Sears the Elder rose each morning at five o'clock, maintaining a typically Puritan outlook on the relationship between success and industry. Unfortunately, an equally widespread Boston custom, the Saturday salt-fish dinner, led to his early death in 1816, at the age of sixty-four. "After a too copious indulgence," wrote his biographer, Robert Winthrop, he died suddenly of "serious indigestion followed by a congestion which proved fatal." The funeral sermon created quite a stir and exemplified yet another current custom, that of early nineteenth century churchmen for the use of Biblical puns. The minister took sudden death as his theme and, as his text, a passage from the first book of Samuel, "There is but a step between us and death," alluding to the fact that Mr. Sears' apoplexy had overcome him as he stepped from his carriage.

His son was only thirty years of age when thus fell upon him the task of managing a fortune. He not only managed it, he increased it. More than that, he created a series of endowments for the benefit of the poor of Boston. By the time of his own death in 1871, the David Sears Charity represented the largest private charitable foundation in the city. His public service extended to politics, and he was a presidential elector as well as a state representative and senator. As early as 1848 he wrote a proposal for the gradual and peaceful abolition of slavery, an institution he found as abhorrent as he did the violence of extremists on both sides of the question.

Three of Clara's older Sears cousins were officers in the Union army, and her mother had witnessed the march of Colonel Robert Gould Shaw and his Negro troops. She often told her daughter about the crowd's enthusiasm as they passed by the State House, Colonel Shaw in the lead on his horse, his men marching behind with proud determination in their eyes. The soldiers' tramp, said Mrs. Sears, "had a sound like a great tornado." Near the State

19

House and not far from Clara's grandfather's mansion on the corner of Beacon and Somerset Streets was St. Gaudens' magnificent memorial to Shaw and his troops.

The childhood memories of Boston which Clara later recorded were without the warmth that suffused her remembrances of idyllic visits to Salem. When Clara and her sister strolled along the tree-shaded mall of Commonwealth Avenue with their nursemaid, they often came upon Grandfather David Sears taking his daily constitutional. While the girls, somewhat in awe of this august figure, excitedly dropped him a curtsey, he in his turn "took off his hat with all the formality accorded elder persons." They thought themselves very grown up to be so greeted, but it was quite in keeping with Victorian custom and, in truth, not nearly as delightful as quiet moments at the knee of their other grandfather, George Peabody.

It was in Salem, with her Peabody grandparents, that Clara's literary curiosity was aroused and stimulated. There was an immediacy there that combined warmth with learning, a personal response unrivaled by all the leather-bound volumes in the well-stocked library of the Sears home at 132 Beacon Street. In the matter of religion, her Peabody grandparents' day-to-day humanitarianism combined with her Sears grandfather's ecumenism to influence Clara toward a strong personal faith enhanced by an unusual tolerance for the beliefs of others. David Sears was known in Boston as much for his nonsectarian religion as for his service in the state legislature and his handsome philanthropies. Toward the end of his life, he built Christ's Church on Colchester Street, Brookline, just outside Boston, culminating at least fifteen years' serious aspiration toward Christian unity. He despised the pretensions and jealousies that typified so many denominations. In his own words,

> It is obvious that men who differ as to the origin of sin or as to the precise nature of the atonement may nevertheless equally love God, and may be alike grateful to him for his mercy, and desire his approval, and seek to know his

will, and adore his infinite perfections. They may differ on many theological questions, and yet may have the same sentiments of devout trust and reverential gratitude, and may equally feel the need of divine help. If they may thus agree in what is essential to devotion, why may they not unite in religious worship - why may they not bow together before that God whom they all adore?

Local clergymen debated which was worse, the audacity of Mr. Sears' religious presumption or the potential diversion of so much of his cash from the coffers of the established church. Wrote Robert Winthrop, "a frown overspread the authoritative features of the Episcopal Bishop of Massachusetts when he learned that the wealthiest layman in his diocese had actually set up a new form of worship."

David Sears retained part of the Episcopal ritual and wrote a prayer book and liturgy that were inspired by the Unitarian William Ellery Channing. He envisioned a church where people of all denominations could gather in a common service, and so they did, but in numbers so small that his ecumenical ideal was not fulfilled. Four ordained ministers succeeded one another in conducting services for the eleven years until Mr. Sears' death, and family members continued to worship at Christ's Church until 1897, but for many years thereafter it was used only for occasional marriages or funerals.

Clara Sears acquired her grandfather's respect for the pursuit of utopian causes and later emulated his religious ecumenism. Though she was a devout Episcopalian, when Harvard University Press failed to include a Unitarian unit in a series of religious books published in 1945, she wrote "quite a severe letter." A year later the press wrote to inform her of the publication of a volume about a Unitarian leader, expressing the hope that "this in some measure will make amends."

She was by then a force to be dealt with, well known for her museums and books chronicling the lost utopias of King Philip's Indian Confederation, Mother Ann's Shakers, and Bronson

Alcott's transcendental experiment. She had also written a scholarly and sympathetic volume, *Days of Delusion*, concerning William Miller, who predicted the end of the world just when Alcott was trying to establish a new Eden. While researching her book on Miller, Miss Sears came across an amusing anecdote which was analogous to Alcott's experience at Fruitlands farm. The crops of the transcendentalists failed because of their excessive attention to philosophical matters; those of many Millerite farms failed because believers deliberately refused to tend them as a demonstration of their faith in the prophecy's fulfillment. In the spring of 1843, said the wife of one convert, "[my] husband had not seen the light, and planted his crops. But now he has found the Lord, and the weeds are higher than the corn, Glory to God."

Although none of her own predecessors was taken in by the revivalist fervor, family letters and diaries corroborated the evidence she was gathering through correspondence and interviews with aging eyewitnesses and through documents previously thought to be of more sentimental than historical value. Great-uncle William Endicott, in a letter to Clara's grandmother, derisively expressed his skepticism when he described a week-long camp meeting of Millerites near Orne's Point in North Salem. "Their success in making converts was, I understand, quite satisfactory, and they proved, as conclusively as the Signs of the Zodiac multiplied by the seeds in a winter squash can prove anything, that this mundane orb of ours...will be extinguished, utterly destroyed, totally annihilated...."

With a kinder view of humanity and the detachment born of distance, Clara Sears sought to understand the origins of these excesses. William Miller, after fourteen years of intense study of the Bible, had reluctantly agreed to preach about his conviction that Christ would come again some time between 1843 and 1844, and that the righteous would rise to meet Him in the air. Although many of his followers carried the message to the point of hysteria, giving away their property and sewing white ascension robes in anticipation of the Day of Judgment, Miller himself was no lunatic. As Miss Sears presented him in *Days of Delusion*, he was a sincere and reasoned believer in his own faulty calculations, a man who lamented the extremes encouraged by self-serving associates but who could do nothing to stem the momentum.

George and Clarissa Peabody had looked on in distress as several townspeople neglected their property or gave it away, convinced they would need it no more. The day before the predicted end of the world, an acquaintance appeared nervously at their door, greatly concerned lest the souls within be found unprepared. "Mr. Peabody! - Mr. Peabody! dear sir! - listen; to-morrow the world is coming to an end! I've come to warn you! My wife and I believe in the prophecy, but my son doesn't, he's obdurate. I've given away my property to him, as we'll not need it any more. Mr. Peabody - you and Mrs. Peabody have been kind to me - you are good people - I hate to think of you and Mrs. Peabody and your children burning in hell-fire - I do - truly I do."

Many Salem believers, arrayed in their ascension robes, awaited the end of the world from the height of Gallows Hill, where the witches were hanged. The deluded friends of the Peabodys chose to wait on their rooftop, quoting scripture as justification. "Let him which is on the house-top not come down." When the prophecy failed, the couple was destitute since their son refused to give back the property, a result that attended many such premature legacies. George Peabody kindly kept track of them for many years and saw to it that they did not die of want. This atmosphere of direct concern for others pervaded the Peabody home and drew Clara irresistibly to it.

The Sears girls used to travel to Salem from Boston by train and liked to pass the time by making up stories about the destinations and probable receptions of fellow passengers. Their own, they knew, could be rivaled by none. They would be met by their grandparents' coachman, John Hayes, who would whisk them to Washington Square in a barouche. This vehicle seated two couples, facing each other, and the half-top over the back seat could be raised or lowered according to the weather. It was a convenient mode of travel, but in no way as showy as Great-grandmother Peabody's yellow coach which boasted a driver with a wig and a footman with powdered hair. Among Clara's later prized possessions was a Russian leather coach cushion filled with eiderdown, which had belonged to Great-grandmother Elizabeth.

Clara's youthful Salem experiences extended beyond elaborate family occasions and quiet but stimulating intellectual moments with her grandparents. Because they also owned a farm in nearby Danvers, she acquired a lifelong love of nature and things rural and owned a farm herself in later years. Her great-grandfather, Joseph Peabody, who feared an attack on Salem during the War of 1812, purchased the Danvers farm as a place of safety for his wife and children. He was the first of many in the family to make improvements, bringing a bit of France to New England by planting an avenue of elms in imitation of the hemlock walk he admired during a trip to Paris and Versailles. When George Peabody inherited the property, it remained a working farm with a resident farmer, a place beloved by his children and grandchildren alike, one they particularly enjoyed in the springtime. Clara thought of it as simple and rustic, even though Mary and William Endicott's parents added a third story and a piazza, and moved onto the property a summerhouse designed in 1793 by Samuel McIntire. This small but elaborate teahouse had large carved figures of a reaper and a milkmaid at the corners of its roof. The public, understandably, began to know the estate as Glen Magna although the family still referred to it as The Farm. When Clara's cousin William and his wife inherited it, they continued to think of it as a rustic place. After all, when dining there one did not have to dress for dinner since it was only a farm. Simple black tie was sufficient.

When Clara, Mamie, and their Endicott cousins were young-sters, The Farm was a showplace by most standards but they felt it to be an ordinary rural New England establishment. They all loved to join their grandmother for picnics there, and memories of such occasions later influenced Clara to want milk from her own cows and apples from her own orchard. The cousins used to watch the evening skies eagerly, trying to guess whether the fol-lowing day would be a good one for a ride to The Farm. Their anticipation ran high when there was a red sky at night. The next day would mean not only sailors' delight but their own as well.

Clara recorded the events of one fine spring day when she and Mamie joined William and Mary for a picnic with their grand-mother.

The dairy was run by two women, old Hannah, as we called her, and Annie McCloys, a dairymaid on the abso-lutely original type, red cheeks, dark hair, dark eyes, and a stout buxom figure.

We always took a special pleasure in seeing Annie, for she gave us such a smiling welcome. In fact it was a great excitement to old Hannah and Annie when they were notified that my grandmother was coming on a picnic. They would busily hustle around getting things ready for us. The quaint low-ceilinged dining room was opened for the occasion, the shades pulled up, and Annie would spread a nice white cloth over the table, and sinking comfortably into a rocking chair my grandmother would say, "Now we'll see what she is going to bring us," and Annie would appear with a tray of freshly made doughnuts and a large apple pie, with some country-made coffee, and a jug of homemade cider.

How well I remember the happy mood we were all in, telling funny stories, and laughing, and having a good time. There was a beautiful great tulip tree with a seat built around it in the middle of what was supposed to be a gar-den, and after our lunch we would go and rest a bit in the spring sunshine, after which we always went down to take a look at the pigs and the cows.

25

No wonder Clara remembered the pleasure and participation of Salem and Danvers days and chose to write of them rather than of Boston in her *Early Personal Reminiscences.* One can only wish that she had also written a first person narrative setting forth the intellectual influences working upon her during summers spent with the Peabodys at the exclusive resort community of Nahant, home also of Longfellow, Lowell, and Agassiz, all of whom were intimates of her grandparents.

CHAPTER 3

The Fatal Sisters

A coy glance, or the wink of an eye can
accomplish wonders. Even the Puritans
could not put the lid on that.

Clara Endicott Sears

Places often assert an influence of their own, beyond the importance of the people associated with them. The Peabody farm introduced an essentially urban Clara Sears to the joys of fields and meadows. After the turn of the century, when she was a grown woman and owned a farm of her own in Harvard, Massachusetts, she wrote a novel set in that rural town and called it *Whispering Pines*. The inspiration of nature was evident throughout.

September sunshine flooded the fields and woods and country lanes. It glistened on the leaves of the trees, - on broad fields of garden truck, - on vines creeping over stone walls; - it crept through the open doors of old barns, glorifying the bales of straw-colored hay and heaps of green fodder piled high in corners; - it lighted up the weather vanes on cupolas and steeples, and played upon the blue waters of the lake and on the swiftly flowing currents of the river; - it filled the earth with gladness, and beautified the whole broad expanse of the Nashua Valley with splashes of gold. The air was pulsating with the rhythmic humming of locusts and crickets and of bees busily gathering honey from tufted gold-enrod and pye weed and from wild asters and Michaelmas daisies growing by the roadsides; - it was one of the days when Nature laughs in the fulness of joy, and as he drove towards the village, Dave Hickson threw his shoulders back and drew a deep breath of sparkling air into his lungs with a sense of exuberant satisfaction.

Miss Sears set all three of her novels in or near the town of Harvard, but several of the poems she wrote in the 1920s and 1930s reflected the influences worked upon her by the wind and waves of Nahant, an exclusive seaside retreat. Her Peabody and Sears grandfathers both owned summer homes there, with magnificent ocean views. Dubbed "cold roast Boston," Nahant was less ostentatious than Newport or Bar Harbor and had the advantage of being but a short commute to the city on the steamboat *Nelly Baker*. Thus, patriarchs bent on business could leave home at 8 a.m. and return in time for a four o'clock dinner. At the Peabodys' table, freshly caught fish were supplemented by squabs and partridges supplied by a Mr. Blood, and the farmer from Glen Magna delivered fresh dairy products, fruit, and vegetables twice weekly. In anticipating the pleasures of Nahant, Clara gave little thought to sailing or salt water bathing although she did enjoy searching the beach for shells and sea anemones. She also tolerated a sociable game of croquet on carefully nurtured expanses of green grass, but she had no interest whatsoever in joining Sears cousins at the vigorous tennis they were so fond of. She looked forward to summer as a time for the leisurely reading of Dumas and Scott, and she probably tried her hand at writing poetry. Friendly critics were nearby in the persons of Grandfather Peabody and Robert Grant, a young man of her set who was ten years her senior and aware of her literary inclinations. Grant became not only a successful lawyer and judge but also a novelist who remained Clara's friend in later life and who continued to encourage her writing. He was a romantic figure to the young Sears girls, addressing them as Miss Clara and Miss Mamie even though they were second cousins. In 1882, he acknowledged Clara's fondness for literary romance by writing a poem to both girls, calling it "The Fatal Sisters."

> Gazing from out the Chamber where I sleep
> I see two ledges crowned with slippery weed
> Known as The Fatal Sisters, for they feed
> On ships and men and all that tempt the deep.
> Ah! Cruel ones a harvest rich ye reap!
> And yet tonight serenely still ye lie
> Shrived in the bright reflection of the sky.
> Was beauty given to make us mortals weep?
>
> I know two maidens wonderfully fair
> Men call them Fatal Sisters and with truth,
> For safe from their enchantment who shall be?
> Rather than suffer disappointment there,
> I should prefer as death-stroke to my youth
> To face their rivals in the raging sea.

George Peabody continued to be an influence on his granddaughter, inclining her compellingly toward the romantic by writing such epics as "The Legend of Swallows' Cave," also a tale of the deep. It recounted the age-old tragedy of the maiden who thought she had lost her lover to the sea and, deranged by grief, cast herself into the waters just at the moment of his return. Based on local Nahant lore, the story was reenacted each summer at the scene of the maiden's leap.

> I hear his voice! - my true love calls!
> He beckons from the sea!
> The torches burn within the Cave!
> Richard! I come to thee!

Clara's pride in her grandfather's talents was renewed yearly by yet another event. In 1869, he composed a hymn for the dedication of Nahant's Union Church and it continued to be sung at the opening of each summer season. Her sense of worth as a member of the Peabody family was reinforced, perhaps even more strongly, by the fact that her grandparents were neighbors and personal friends of Henry Wadsworth Longfellow. It would have been a privilege beyond price if she could have joined them for afternoon tea. Perhaps she did.

Both Clara and Clarissa delighted in learning Longfellow's poems by heart. One which he wrote about the evening chimes of nearby Lynn appealed greatly to Clara and she was fond of reciting portions.

> Borne on the evening wind across the crimson twilight
> O'er land and sea ye rise and fall
> O bells of Lynn.

Years later, this influence was reflected in lines from her own "Vesper Bells in the Nashaway Valley."

> At eventide
> When light is fading,
> And the sunset tints
> Are shading
> Into violet and grey,-
> Across the valley
> Their sweet pealing
> Soothes the heart
> With magic healing
> Like a song
> From far away.-
> But they always
> Peal for me
> Like mystic bells
> Of memory.

Clara's love of literature was as well known to her parents as to her grandparents. Therefore, when the Sears family returned to Boston for the winter season of 1882, they reluctantly allowed nineteen-year-old Clara to attend a lecture by Oscar Wilde. He was staying at the Hotel Vendome, and the "Hub" was quite titillated by the event. As Clara later wrote, "The good ladies of Beacon Hill did not quite know what to do about it, for rumors had come over here that he was not as straight-laced as he should be." Smothered laughter accompanied Mr. Wilde's appearance on stage, and Clara was torn between staring at him and glancing surreptitiously around to see who was there and who would therefore know she was there.

Years later, when she was in her nineties and herself wintering at the Vendome, the proprietor gave her access to the hotel's old registers so that she could compile a volume of short biographies about artists and statesmen who had stayed there during the 1880s and 1890s. In recalling her attendance at Oscar Wilde's lecture she wrote

> I don't know what I expected to see, but what I did see came with a shock of surprise. Instead of a young man flourishing his poetship, Wilde came on to the stage with a quiet dignity that was wholly unlooked-for. One felt a faint wave of disappointment filtering through the audience. But in another moment astonishment over Wilde's attire met with complete satisfaction - they were seeing what they had come to see. He wore knee breeches of black satin bound in at the knees by large rhinestone buckles. His coat was a black velvet cutaway worn open to show a gorgeous yellow brocaded waistcoat. He wore his hair like the poets of the day - rather long and parted in the middle. It was chestnut brown in color and exceedingly well groomed. To complete his attire there was pinned to the lapel of his coat a monstrous great sunflower looking as big as his head. It was the fashionable boutonniere among the aesthetes of the day.
>
> We had not seen anything of this sort here, and it caused considerable merriment. Sounds like smothered laughter could be heard here and there, but when Wilde approached the footlights and began to speak in an unmistakably English well-modulated voice, a sudden silence spread through the crowd. Here again was something it had

not expected. He spoke very easily. There was no effort. What he had to say had no high-sounding or aesthetic tinge to it.

The Hotel Vendome had opened on April 3, 1872, and a large addition was finished a few years later. It was the first hotel to be built on the newly filled-in Back Bay, the third in the country to boast of using Thomas Edison's new invention, the electric light. On walks as young children, Clara and Mamie used to urge their nursemaid along to the Dartmouth Street entrance, eager for a glimpse of the arriving or departing dowager ladies of the Victorian Lunch Club. These elderly women wore silks and velvets from Paris, glittering diamond brooches, and invariably, black velvet bonnets from which sprang waving white ostrich plumes. No less intriguing were the gentlemen who arrived at the same entrance, whether by foot or in a fine equipage, in order to have their whiskers trimmed according to the latest mode by their favorite barber, Gus Schneider.

As they matured, the girls became more interested in catching glimpses of theatrical luminaries who were staying at the hotel. Clara was well up on their comings and goings. It was common practice then to keep a scrapbook along the lines of one's interest, and her pages were replete with reviews of theatrical performances and notices of the stars' social schedules. In December of 1880, she saw Sarah Bernhardt play in Racine's *Phaedra* and witnessed for herself the cheering crowds which inevitably pursued the Divine Sarah back to her suite at the Vendome. Since the play was a true classic, Mr. and Mrs. Sears had the wisdom to let their daughter attend even though, being fluent in French, she would be able to understand all the nuances of the heroine's tragic passion for her stepson.

Whenever possible, Clara found a way to relate family members to literary or theatrical events. The Norwegian violinist Ole Bull had spent an hour or so with George Peabody in his upstairs retreat at Washington Square. The singer Adelina Patti was a protégée of Mr. Bull so Clara felt, as she put it, an extra thrill when she went to hear her in *La Dame aux Camelias* in 1886. Actually, Bull's visit to her grandfather was not of great significance except to George Peabody and to Clara, who felt that such a courtesy from a world-renowned musician enhanced what she felt to be her grandfather's already lustrous artistic standing. Ole Bull was introduced to George Peabody by a mutual friend, and the maestro was kind enough to praise Mr. Peabody's Amati violin after playing a few bars upon it.

During an 1895 journey to England with her mother, Clara again heard Adelina Patti sing, and her journal entry for June 24 shows a knowledge of voice as well as the frankness which was a lifelong hallmark.

> I went to hear Patti sing in *Don Giovanni.* While her voice has lost its power it is exquisite in quality and she is such an artist that she knows just how to manage it so that it is never forced or anything but beautiful. The opera house was completely full and all the swells of London seemed to be there. The jewels there were gorgeous but I did not see one good looking woman wearing them. The lack of beauty in the modern English woman is most striking and paint and powder is so universally used that one no longer sees the fresh pink cheeks so associated with English women. The men are splendidly handsome.

Clara Sears appreciated a good-looking man. She was not a flirt, however, and even as a debutante did not care to waste her time on males whose intelligence was not up to snuff. Although her seriousness discouraged escorts from romantic advances, she was nonetheless a popular belle and accustomed to being described by the press as striking, if not beautiful. She always dressed carefully and tastefully, with as much concern for the public response to her appearance as for her own pleasure in wearing becoming gowns. When a child, she had observed the grown-ups. Now it was her turn to be observed. One wonders how she felt about the measured praise once accorded her by the *Boston Sunday Herald.* "While Miss Clara Sears would not attract so much attention as one meets her on the street or at a tea, yet for evening attire there is probably no woman that can equal her." In the hyperbole typical of the era, the reporter went on to refer to Miss Sears as a "veritable goddess" in her ball gowns of pink, and he marveled that she could be a beauty even in yellow, a most difficult color to wear.

Clara regarded her debut as merely the customary thing to do. She enjoyed the parties and the attention but, to the disappointment of her mother and father, was not looking for a husband. Quite the contrary. In her parents' union, happy though it was, she observed a narrowing preoccupation with the world of society, and she suspected that a husband would almost surely perpetuate the Victorian dependence that she was beginning to find restrictive. She and Cousin Mary decided that each would remain single unless she found exactly the right man. They were joined in this resolution by a third cousin of their age, Fanny Mason, daughter of Fanny (Peabody) and Powell Mason of Commonwealth Avenue.

The pleasure of dancing was not denied the girls after their debuts, for there was in Boston a unique social institution known as the Subscription Assembly. Assemblies were expressly designed by the dancing master, Count Lorenzo Papanti, so that the social elite could enjoy the polka, waltz, and quadrille well beyond dancing school and debutante years. Adults of all ages could attend, and women did not need to be escorted. Their safe return home was guaranteed by trustworthy hack drivers of Kenny and Clark's Charles Street stables. Into the 1900s, Clara was often in the receiving line at Subscription Assemblies. She enjoyed them, enjoyed being seen at them, and felt no need for an escort when dance cards could be filled to overflowing without regard to age and without commitment to any particular swain. She remained open to romance but neither sought nor required it. She had been a popular belle and continued to sparkle in the company of men all her life, not to attract them, but because she felt they tended to be infinitely more interesting than women.

34

In 1883, Mamie Sears married Frank Shaw, and it was at about that time that Mrs. Sears pasted "Quite Too Dreadful" into her scrapbook.

> The atmosphere was balmy,
>   But suddenly the air
> Grew chill as if an iceberg
>   Had wandered from its lair.
> What caused the cold sensation
>   Of a nipping Arctic blast?
> Why, a frigid Boston spinster
>   Just then went sailing past.

No doubt she thought this bit of newspaper doggerel more amusing than prophetic. While recognizing that Clara's goals were at odds with those of the social world she frequented, she had not given up hope that her younger daughter would marry one day. The only possible career either could consider for a moment was teaching, but that was really out of the question. Clara did not have the patience even had such an occupation been socially acceptable. She claimed to have given up the idea when she was unable to teach two young neighbor children that cows give milk and chickens lay eggs. In a similarly facetious vein, she made light of her musical interests. Although she played the violin and took voice lessons, she did not have the musical gifts of her mother or her sister. She told an interviewer for the *Boston Transcript* that she became a self-professed critic because Mamma and Mamie practiced so much there was no time left for her, implying that they were more proficient. Such comments were not the result of modesty. Clara was trying not to let it become apparent how much she wanted to succeed.

It is impossible to know how realistically Clara Sears pursued thoughts of a music or teaching career. Such notions probably dwelt in the nebulous realms of yearning, but in acknowledging them at all she indicated that her search for a career began early if not vigorously. Throughout her twenties and thirties she found enough to occupy her although she was confident that ultimately she would "do something more constructive [than] going about, luncheon here, dinner there, dancing and entertainments."

At one dinner party she had some thoughts which, if articulated, would have assured those seated near her that she was the embodiment of the frigid Boston spinster. Her chance dinner companion was a man she considered to be about as fast as one could find. She thought him "too hardened in the ways of the world ever to reform or appreciate the good things in life." That he was an agreeable talker and handsome as well made him "a direct menace." Curiosity prompted Miss Sears to ask him the name of the most beautiful woman he had ever known. When he responded with that of a mutual acquaintance who was undeniably ugly, she "flared up in a fury of wrath," believing he was making a cruel jest. Her face flushed with anger; but instead of bursting forth in an immediate torrent of protest, she looked at him and saw to her surprise that the expression on his face had softened.

It seems that this woman, a member of a hospital visiting board, had befriended him when he was alone and seriously ill. Although she was initially reluctant to sit with him because of his reputation, she stayed by his bed for hours at a time, calmed him, and listened to his surprising outpourings of unhappiness. In return, though he "well knew how the world looks upon a woman so lacking in its estimate of beauty," she became to him the most beautiful woman he had ever known.

Although Clara Sears tended to keep her guard up where men were concerned, she acknowledged that, in this instance, she had been overly quick in her judgment. The woman concerned was particularly well known to her, hence her haste to condemn the man. Both women were volunteers at Carney Hospital and gave generously of time and money. Miss Sears belonged to the hospital's Ladies Aid Society for sixteen years, from the age of twenty-five, and she served for many years as its president. It was to her liking that the press paid less attention to her good works than to her ball gowns. In her charities she was quietly following the precedent of Searses and Peabodys and was thus already involved in matters of more substance than dances and dinners.

Clara, Mary, and Fanny continued to share a general skepticism about men although Clara had learned a useful lesson and became somewhat less hasty in her criticism of the opposite sex. Though the cousins did not condemn marriage in the abstract, they staunchly agreed that they would not marry for marriage's sake, nor did they. Miss Sears was to have a bittersweet taste of romance in the 1890s; Miss Mason devoted her adult life to music and was an important benefactor of the Boston Symphony; Miss Endicott found love unexpectedly at the British Embassy in Washington. When her father, Judge Endicott, was appointed secretary of war in the Cleveland administration, the family left Salem for a sunny three-story mansion on Sixteenth Street in Washington, where the press pounced upon the opportunity to comment on this "Puritan maiden" who was "Boston to the tips of her fingers." It was reported, accurately no doubt, that she bore herself proudly, almost disdainfully. Reporters noted that Mary Endicott was highly cultured, "wore an expression of intellectuality," liked to talk philosophy, and had even written poetry. Though she was unquestionably pretty, she was referred to as "a beautiful hyperborean ice queen" and "was not a great belle in the sense of being popular with the men of her set, simply because her treatment of their innocent attempts to advance in her acquaintance was solidly frigid." Washington reporters had a field day with their equivalent of "Quite Too Dreadful."

Romance was in the air, however. President Cleveland had recently married the attractive and popular Miss Folsom, who became very close to Mrs. Endicott. In fact, during Mrs. Cleveland's first visit to Boston, in November of 1886, she was accompanied by the Endicotts, and they all stayed with the Powell Masons at 211 Commonwealth Avenue. Young Fanny, Mary, and Clara were agog over the visit, and a most ungenteel curiosity manifested itself as the Masons' neighbors began to pull draperies

37

back from windows and to push furniture aside in order to obtain unobstructed glimpses of President Cleveland's young bride. She arrived by train on a Saturday in a cold November rainstorm, stopping at Kneeland Street rather than the expected Columbus Street station so as to avoid the great crush of expected onlookers. One disappointed shop girl commented, "She ought to allow herself to be looked at because the people all take such delight in doing her homage."

The following day Mrs. Cleveland was gracious and smiling though her way was impeded by the crowds awaiting her arrival at Trinity Church for a Sunday service by the Reverend Phillips Brooks. In the afternoon, the Masons resorted to subterfuge in order to entertain their guest with a ride to Brookline. A Berlin carriage with silver-trimmed trappings, drawn by a pair of bang-tailed bays, arrived at 211 Commonwealth Avenue within minutes of being ordered from Kenny and Clark's, but word spread quickly, and no sooner had Mr. Mason escorted the First Lady to her seat than the avenue was full of equestrians, and the neighbors across the street were beguiled by a white chapel cart containing four dashing swells. "Two young ladies, members of the household," reported next day's newspaper, had joined Powell Mason and Mrs. Cleveland and were no doubt torn as to which was the more exciting, the scene within or the scene without the carriage. In all likelihood, the two young women were Fanny and Mary, but Clara surely heard all about the subsequent ruse. As soon as the footman closed the carriage door, the coachman wheeled his horses in the opposite direction from the Mill Dam, toward which they had been heading, and drove rapidly up Commonwealth Avenue to Exeter Street. The trick rid the party of their unwanted escort and merely reversed the planned itinerary. Mrs. Cleveland was shown the State House first, and then they turned around for the drive to Brookline and Longwood. She pronounced herself delighted with her tour of Boston even though the tide was low and the flats of the Charles River in reality rather ugly.

President Cleveland's visit was even more hectic than that of his wife since his appearances were arranged for maximum rather than minimum public exposure. At 3:00 a.m. on Monday morning the presidential train arrived at Springfield, where a special car for his Massachusetts escort was deftly attached so as not to disturb his slumber. Governor Robinson received him in Boston at 6:00 a.m., and they were driven off through great crowds in a barouche drawn by four matched dapple grays. The Vendome was his headquarters for the day. After breakfasting there, he was driven to Cambridge, amid cheering, clapping, and waving of handkerchiefs, for his part in Harvard's 250th anniversary celebration. In the afternoon, this "plain, hearty man of the people" was taken to Faneuil Hall where he shook hands with those from all walks of life, from state officials, to men who came from nearby butchers' stalls still dressed in stained white aprons, to young women on their way home from work with lunch baskets and work bags still in hand. By the time he had to return to the Vendome for a quick supper and an evening reception, he had shaken hands with over two thousand people. The police had formed a human aisle, large at the beginning and small at the end so that, pushed with fearful force by the people behind, when a well-wisher reached the small opening, "he or she popped out like a pea from a blow gun. Sometimes they came out whole and sometimes they didn't as was proved later on by a curious collection of ribbons, bows, neckties, cloak ornaments, etc., on the floor when the hall was vacated."

Secretary Endicott, being a Democrat, was more attuned to the working classes than were the Searses, who were Republicans. Clara Sears, in giving a speech to the Massachusetts Society of Mayflower Descendants many years later, at the age of seventy, articulated her own blue-blooded position rather frankly. Though ecumenical in religious outlook and an early champion of Native Americans, in the sanctuary of her own kind she admitted her social prejudices but again evidenced her willingness to alter her views when circumstances warranted. Her comments concerned the occasion of the return to Boston of the frigate "Old Ironsides." The streets were crowded with celebrating masses of people, and the ceremony began with the singing of an anthem Miss Sears had written called "Hymn to America." As she looked at the throngs of Italians, Poles, and Irish, thoughts of the Mayflower Pilgrims came to her mind and she was at first distressed to see so many foreign looking faces which bore no resemblance to "our old original stock." She sought out and was comforted by fellow Mayflower descendants who had a "home-like familiar look," until the enthusiasm of so many ethnic groups worked a change upon her.

> Then it came over me that history was forever repeating itself in a country like this. These were pilgrims from faraway places, - people who were not satisfied with the lack of opportunity in the countries where they were born, and had sought our shores, confident that here they would find liberty and prosperity, and the joy of a new start in life. So I began to feel differently about them, and as if they after all had some right to be here.

Despite such sentiments, her guest lists seldom included anyone of other than English ethnic origins. In Washington in 1887, on the other hand, many of the representatives of foreign governments to whom Clara was introduced were quite acceptable. She joined Cousin Mary there for a fortnight of diplomatic receptions at the turn of the new year, and Mrs. Sears surely did not neglect to point out that many of the diplomats were eligible bachelors. As in Boston, Clara's appearances at balls captivated the Washington press corps, and articles began to appear expressing admiration of the fetching costumes that set off "her exquisite figure" for two full weeks of parties, each new gown "a becoming casket for so much beauty."

Society pages savored details of decoration and dress, and reporters gushed over a New Year's reception that Clara and Mary attended at the White House. On the mantel in the Green Room was a floral flag composed of red and white camellias, in which a center square of carnations and mignonette proclaimed the date. Mary's gown was of "heliotrope cloth, trimmed with heliotrope of a lighter shade," and she "looked the ideal Puritan maiden." The girls were annoyed by the continual harping on the Puritan theme, especially when local wags suggested that a charming dessert for a cabinet dinner would be pears from a tree planted in Salem by Governor Endicott himself more than two hundred years before and still bearing. Better yet, the pears should be "wrapped in nappery spun and woven by a daughter of the house and laid in a basket of twigs from the old trees round the house."

Clara and Mary had more amusing things to do than spin and weave, however. With their background, upbringing, and European travels, they were excited but not awed by the diplomatic rounds of Washington. When they assisted in receiving at a reception given by the Endicotts, Clara knew that she would not be referred to as Puritan, at least not in the matter of dress. She wore a gown of "white brocaded satin, slashed at the right side over a white satin petticoat and bordered with open-work bullion braid. The corsage was with low neck and short sleeves, finished with the same bullion braid. In front a full illusion puff from either shoulder was caught in the center with a pansy of dead gold, with diamond center."

It was the "hyperborean ice queen," however, who succumbed to love. A grand fete was given at the British legation by Sir Lionel Sackville-West, to introduce his youngest daughter, Amelia, to society. After general dancing and a midnight supper, the cotillion itself began. Forty couples danced various elaborate figures, each with a theme and corresponding favors more elaborate than anything the girls had seen at Boston Assemblies. In the first figure, for example, there were Japanese umbrellas with long ribbons, each one having seven different colors. Bells of corresponding colors were held by the gentlemen, who chose their partners by the colors of the ribbons.

Because of their shared reticence towards the opposite sex, until that evening at least, Clara's attention to the dancing was more than a little distracted by Cousin Mary's unusual behavior. To Clara's amazement, upon Mary's introduction to the British MP from Birmingham, Joseph Chamberlain, both he and she seemed to lose all sense of being in a public place. That fact did not escape reporters of the social scene.

> After a little conversation and a stroll through the rooms they took a seat upon one of the luxurious sofas in the hallway, and here, with the gaily dressed throng passing and repassing every moment, they remained for the greater portion of the evening so mutually absorbed with each other as to be seemingly oblivious of the flight of time or their surroundings.

Others also noticed Joseph and Mary's undeniable attraction to one another that evening and throughout Mr. Chamberlain's short stay in Washington. Newspapers began to refer to Mary as "very English in appearance and manner," holding Puritan references in temporary abeyance. The Endicotts, they said, would rejoice at an English connection for their daughter because they were proud of their fine old ancestry. The latter was true, the former much too simple. Mary and her family did not immediately look with favor upon the idea of her moving to England, which such a connection would require. Furthermore, Joseph Chamberlain had been twice widowed and was thirty years older than Mary. On the other hand, he was wealthy, extremely handsome, youthful appearing, and obviously devoted to her. Before his return to England they made social calls together, thus encouraging rumors of an engagement, but close friends and relatives kept whatever they knew of the matter to themselves.

In one respect, Mary differed from Clara in her views of matrimony. Mary felt that she could maintain her own individuality within marriage if it were with a suitable man of importance. She meant to bring prominence, not subjugation, to her role as Mrs. Joseph Chamberlain. That she succeeded was confirmed by the gold medal presented to her by Queen Victoria on her Diamond Jubilee, an honor usually reserved for members of reigning royal families.

Before the end of January 1887, Joseph returned to his duties in England, carrying on his courtship largely by correspondence, while Mary and her family considered the consequences of an irrevocable return to the country of her ancestors. Over a year and a half passed in indecision, but on November 7, 1888, Joseph sailed for the United States to claim his bride. In Washington, on November 15, he put on his Prince Albert coat and fastened to his lapel a boutonniere of white violets instead of the orchid he generally wore. Outside, the sky was leaden and a misty rain was falling, "regular English weather," marveled the newspapers. Given the inclement day and the Endicotts' efforts to ensure privacy, there was no gawking crowd, but Mr. Chamberlain sought to guarantee anonymity by ordering an inconspicuous equipage for the ride to the church. The livery was less conservative than Kenny and Clark's of Boston and sent instead "a bran-new, satin-lined vehicle" drawn by spirited horses. The bridegroom returned it impatiently and demanded in its place the worst looking vehicle available. Given to terse and colorful analogies, he sarcastically commented, "If there is an old yellow beast in your stables put him before the carriage. When I ask for an egg, I don't wish to be served with two."

Mary, meanwhile, was already at St. John's Episcopal Church, simply dressed in a traveling costume of gray camel's hair. Rather than a bouquet, she carried three Puritan rose buds tied with streamers of white satin ribbon. The wedding ceremony was extremely simple, befitting Mary's temperament and the fact that Joseph had been previously married. President and Mrs.

Cleveland, still newlyweds themselves, were among the first to arrive and were followed by cabinet families and a few friends. Though there were no bridesmaids, Clara, Fanny Mason, and two other unmarried cousins sat together during the service and were delighted with Mr. Chamberlain's gifts to each of them, rings set with diamonds and sapphires. In the church vestibule, after the ceremony, the four girls watched with affection as a waiting maid wrapped Mary in a long white lamb's wool boa, which Joseph lovingly tucked close to her throat before escorting her to the waiting carriage. No old hackney, but a fine coupe awaited the newlyweds, and Joseph Chamberlain's "active, springing step gave no suspicion that he had passed half a century."

The wedding was a happy event, but it marked the beginning of a series of losses in Clara's life. With her marriage, Mary did take up lifelong residence in England and became a British subject. The courses of the two young women took very different turns. The one constant in their lives was the Peabody farm in Danvers, the scene of so many childhood pleasures and now Mary's home base during her annual visits to America. Joseph Chamberlain was well known in England for his horticultural expertise, and as Mary's husband he contributed to the continuing improvement of Glen Magna's grounds, personally planning and spading beds for flower and shrubbery gardens. He and Mary had twenty-six years of married life before he died; and her stepsons, Austin and Neville, continued to keep in touch with Peabody and Endicott connections.

It was but two years after Mary Endicott's wedding that Mamie Sears Shaw died of tuberculosis, not long after the birth of her daughter, Miriam. Her son, Frank, was only a toddler, and her first-born had died in infancy. Destiny did not deal kindly with Mamie. Only eight years after Robert Grant wrote his poem to the "Fatal Sisters," the eldest was dead and Mrs. Sears found consolation in copying out some lines by the British poet Felicia Hemans.

Calm on the bosom of thy God
  Fair Spirit - rest thee now!
E'en while with us thy footsteps trod
  His seal was on thy brow.
Dust to its narrow house beneath
  Soul to its place on high
They that have seen thy look in death
  No more may fear to die.

There was more grief yet to come, for Knyvet Sears died suddenly a year later, while vacationing at Nahant. A newspaper tribute from a friend summed up his character.

> In the death of Knyvet Winthrop Sears, his friends have sustained a loss that will always be felt. Of modest and retiring disposition, with a sensitive temperament which caused him to shun all forms of publicity, his rare qualities were known and appreciated but by a few. Under an exterior of reserve and apparent indifference, lay a warm heart, a delightful sense of humor and a candid and generous spirit.... He had a high sense of honor, and that rare self control which is the finishing touch of the gentleman. He never allowed himself to show anger, and it was simply impossible for him to be discourteous. Unfitted by temperament and education for practical affairs, his comments on men and measures were often keen and discriminating, and no one gave more generous applause to those who seemed to him superior in ability or enterprise. Such a character is worthy of all remembrance, and hence this brief and imperfect tribute from a friend.

In 1892, the year following the death of her father, both of Clara's Peabody grandparents passed away, George in January and a grieving Clarissa three months later. That these two deaths were in the natural course of events did not assuage the grief of Clara and her mother. The old Peabody mansion became the Bertram Home for Aged Men, and only with the passage of years could Clara write in her *Early Personal Reminiscences* that the old gentlemen now living there were no doubt content and perhaps even heard echoes of the happy family life that had been lived there for so many years. "If I had emotional courage enough to cross that threshold, I am sure I would hear far-away strains of my grandfather's violin and would catch a sudden vision of my grandmother sitting in her chair looking out upon St. Peter's Church at sunset and listening to it chiming, as day closes."

Clara was twenty-nine years of age in 1892. The loss of so many loved ones in so few years determined her to give all possible care and attention to her mother. At the time it was an overwhelming and heartfelt desire. With the passage of years she offered a less emotional response in *Whispering Pines*. Marcia, the heroine, feels bound by the obligation put upon her by her dying father, to care for her mother, denying all personal considerations. Marcia therefore refuses the suitor she loves but in so doing asks herself, "Was it Duty calling? - or was it her Mother? - or both?" For Miss Sears it was both duty and love, and it is possible that a third element played a part in the real-life decision. With Mrs. Sears to care for, Clara could respectably remain single.

CHAPTER 4

The Pergolas

*It was this tendency to take things seriously
that kept Myrtle Stone somewhat apart from the
young folk who were prone to give and take
without troubling themselves with questions
they could not answer.*

The Romance of Fiddler's Green
Clara Endicott Sears

By inclination and upbringing, Clara Sears imposed control
over deeply felt personal emotions, rarely allowing them expression lest they expose too much to public view. She was as devas-
tated as her mother by the deaths of Mamie, her father, and her
grandparents; but she was the comforter, not the comforted. In
those grief-filled years before her thirtieth birthday, she came into
her own as an adult companion to her mother and began to take
over the conduct of her life. There was little overt change.
Mamma still managed their various households, but Clara no
longer felt obliged to account for her activities. She gave high
priority to her mother's welfare; and a mutual, comfortable
understanding of their differences began to underlie their successful relationship. By the turn of the century, however, Clara's

own life had become badly out of balance. Her innate intensity had no outlet, emotional or professional; her self-control became a liability.

The attitudes of her hero and heroine in *Whispering Pines* partially paralleled her own situation, and she must have identified with both. The heroine, Marcia, refuses her lover in order to devote herself to her mother. Dave, upon being thus turned down, abandons himself temporarily to an innocent attraction to a wild gypsy girl and to the same obsession with painting for which his father had been ostracized from conventional society. Dave Hickson loves nature and wants passionately to portray it in oils. In the end, he balances passion with control, making a socially respectable profession of his art by becoming a landscape architect. By 1914, similarly, Miss Sears had become a preservationist and writer of history, thus accommodating her literary inclinations to social expectations. Each found an emotional outlet by depicting the varied moods of nature, she in poetry, he in painting.

In *Whispering Pines*, Dave sees woods and fields with the author's eyes.

He walked about, keeping a watchful eye out to see what he could discover, and after taking a drink at the spring he penetrated up into the wood, examining the growth of the pine trees as he went, and taking note of the amount of water flowing in the little brook that had become partly choked with dead twigs and leaves, and so on until he found himself up on the hill at the boundary wall beyond which there was a broad clearing. Here he came to a stand-still and gazed with admiration at the sight that met his eyes. A dark green belt of ancient pines stretched along the North side of the clearing, and nestling close to them was a foreground made up of great broad groups of stag-horn sumacs which a slight frost the night before had turned to a brilliant scarlet that now blazed and glowed and pulsated in the sunshine, while masses and masses of every variety of goldenrod spread like a yellow blanket of color around them, and over the clearing, and in and out among the grey granite rocks that protruded from the wild unreclaimed land. A sudden thought of his father's canvases and palettes and brushes and tubes of old paint that lay hidden in the loft of his uncle's barn flashed through his mind. He felt his pulses quicken. A reckless desire to defy everybody and to give in to the craving that was harassing him swept through him with a mighty force, - he seemed unable and even unwilling to stem it.

Miss Sears' love of nature, acquired at Glen Magna, was further nurtured by yet another rural scene. She and her mother spent autumns and springs at Riverdale Farm, their country estate in Groton, Massachusetts. The uninterrupted western view took in a semicircle of mountains in the distance, including the rocky summit of Mt. Monadnock in New Hampshire. She was to have mixed feelings about Groton in future years. It was here that she found the strength to make an overt declaration of her independence, in 1910, but it was also here that she found herself unexpectedly attracted to a married man.

Jim Lawrence graduated from Harvard in 1874, was married in 1875, traveled widely in Europe, and in 1876 took up residence on Farmers' Row in Groton, where he immersed himself in farming and stock raising on an extensive scale. He was a longstanding member of the American Shropshire Sheep Association, the Massachusetts Horticultural Society, and the Guernsy and Ayrshire Societies. He was also a director of several manufacturing companies and a member of the Massachusetts House of Representatives. He and his wife, Estelle, were shipboard companions of Clara and her mother when they sailed for Europe in the spring of 1895. Since Jim was safely married, Clara allowed herself to be more relaxed than usual and realized too late that she felt more for him than she should. She came to enjoy and long for his companionship. Proximity to Jim when she was in Groton was a source of joy at first; ultimately, it was an important motivation in the sale of Riverdale Farm.

On May 8, 1895, Clara and her mother, with their personal maid, Eliza, boarded the *Teutonic* bound for Liverpool. Clara no longer followed along as a dependent but was, instead, a participant in the necessary planning and preparation. The main purpose of their voyage was to visit Mary Chamberlain. The journal Clara kept during the trip, the earliest remaining example of her writing, shows her to have been a keen observer with a nice sense of the ridiculous and a knack for fixing her subjects in words as well as on film. She was still interested in photography, taking pictures during the day and penning her impressions at night. Clearly delighted to be having some fun, she expressed herself with a joyous spontaneity that was never to be repeated. Clara went about a good bit with Jim and Estelle, and it was his company in particular that accounted for her lightness of spirit. That she did not destroy her diary suggests that she considered her pleasure in the Lawrences' company to be innocent. Only later did she realize that she had fallen in love.

The week-long ocean voyage was smooth, wrote Clara, "with the exception of one day when the *Teutonic* stood on her head most of the time." She frequently remarked on the state of her mother's health and noted that Mamma was "particularly well" even during the rough day. On May 14, they sighted the Irish coast and that evening remained late on deck to watch the lights on shore. At Liverpool the next day, Clara poked about the antique shops, taking Eliza along as was her practice when otherwise unescorted. Clara had long been a collector. Years before, when she was very young and was given some francs to buy a doll in Paris, she chose instead a tiny antique pitcher. She was no more fond of dolls then than she was of babies later.

On Thursday, May 16, Jim engaged a carriage, and they all had a comfortable ride to London. At Rugby, a basket lunch of hot chops, bread, and Medoc was put in, and they were all in fine fettle when they arrived at the Albermarle Hotel in Picadilly. The festive mood was short-lived, however, because they discovered Mary Chamberlain awaiting them with the news that Mrs. Sears' sister, Fanny Mason, had died. It is interesting to compare Clara's journal accounts with those of her mother during this trip. In this instance Mamma wrote calmly, "Mary Chamberlain called and told me of dear Fran's death the previous Friday, May 10th. She had been cabled to tell me of it." Clara, on the other hand, wrote that the news had overwhelmed her mother and that the shock would surely make her ill. She and Mary must take her as soon as possible to Highbury, the Chamberlains' country place near Birmingham. Somehow the two younger women managed first to dash off to White's, which Mary considered the best dressmaker in London, to order for Clara a short black dress and a low-necked black satin for evening. The frocks were whipped up in a day and delivered before their Saturday departure for Highbury.

Clara found much to photograph and was delighted with the grounds at Highbury, which were ingeniously laid out so that they were able to stroll about for two hours without retracing their steps. As she wrote in her journal, "There is a charming pond where ducks and a white swan add greatly to the picturesque effect. The banks are overgrown with rhododendrons which are in full bloom and many flowering trees and shrubs so that the effect was lovely. A moor hen...had built her nest in the rushes and we would watch for her to see her teach her little fluffy balls of chickens to swim."

She thought Joseph Chamberlain's greenhouses were a marvel. He explained his theories on the growing of orchids and showed his guests half a dozen glasshouses leading out from a central glass corridor and filled with exotic plants. The fragrant jasmine was in bloom, and Clara was intrigued by an artificial stream in the fern house. The three-day stay restored her peace of mind, whether her mother's needed restoring or not.

Mrs. Sears' journal for this 1895 trip contains many short entries such as, "Mary most kind and devoted," and, back in London, "Mary came this afternoon and took Clara off." Sometimes the three went about together; sometimes Clara and Mary went

51

off alone in the Chamberlain barouche to see the sights and to shop. Mrs. Sears had a great many friends of her own in London; mother and daughter allowed one another freedom to pursue their own interests. In the evenings, she and Clara frequently dined with Mary and Joseph at their town house, 40 Prince's Gardens, where food was often neglected for talk. Austin and Neville Chamberlain, as Clara noted, "were imbued with politics from their early youth," but she was more absorbed by people than policy. When she went with the Chamberlains to a meeting of the Women's Liberal Unionist Association, where Joseph was one of the speakers, she took full advantage of her seat on the platform and recounted the vagaries of behavior rather than the political views of the speakers.

> The Duke of Devonshire spoke first and opened the meeting very well. He is decidedly ponderous and his manner was rather vague but this I attributed to the Duchess of Devonshire coming to the edge of the platform and whispering in a loud whisper "My dear what *have* you done to your cravat? It is all under one ear!" Of course, the Duke being human and having feelings akin to man, could not hear such an announcement with unconcern and I felt when I heard his railing at the Gladstonians that in his heart he was railing at the pin that had come out of his cravat and allowed it to assume a rakish appearance. Miss Fawcett spoke next and enlivened the audience considerably. I was much impressed by her complete self-possession and easy delivery. She did extremely well and was much applauded. Towards the end she became a little less strong because the Duchess of Westminster poked her in the back and whispered that it was time to stop, which certainly must have been disconcerting and I noticed she wavered a good deal and made several unnecessary assertions.

When Mr. Chamberlain rose to speak, people stood on their chairs and waved their hats. Clara was impressed by the clarity of his points and the authority in his voice, which was "strong and ringing without being too loud." She readily understood why he was "such a power in the House of Commons" and found his sarcasm "searching to a degree."

In writing her journal, Clara was sharpening her powers of observation as well as showing increasing signs of the romanticism evidenced in her later historical novels. This was particularly true while they were in France. Toward the end of May, the two women crossed the English Channel. They began their stay in Rouen, planning to meet the Lawrences later, in Paris. As in all places they visited, Clara and Mrs. Sears both displayed a thorough knowledge of historical background. Clara went without her mother to the tower where Joan of Arc had been imprisoned, "as Mamma felt tired." An old keeper took her to the chamber in which Joan was tortured and then to her cell, at the end of which a narrow slit "let a ray of light in and a little air." The keeper allowed her to go into the cell alone, and as she stood near the slit, pondering the agonies of the Maid of Orleans, her attention was taken by the song of a bird. Looking out through the narrow opening, she saw a "big purple fleur de lys nodding in at me. I thought whoever planted it there must have had a good heart."

Traveling in an open carriage through the "land of Dumas" from Rouen to Paris, Clara found that the little villages clearly recalled favorite books to her mind. As they neared the Hotel Winsor, on the Rue de Rivoli, she and her mother

> felt as if we were in a dream, for Paris is so familiar to us and so full of memories of Papa and Mamie. It was like coming into a thoughtless beehive. If London seems a whirl of business, there is a purpose in it all that impresses one. Here everyone is going recklessly any way and every way. The fiacres dart in every direction and apparently have a special providence to look after them, for no skill in driving prevents them from smashing into the first thing that comes along.... There are bicycles everywhere. Men and women have gone mad on the subject and all the women wear

knickerbockers. They look like wasps with their small waists, large hips, and little heads. I can only call them odious to look at.

She photographed them anyway.

Though she would have nothing to do with knickerbockers or those who wore them, she did copy one Parisian custom. The women "held up lace sunshades because they were new and pretty with no regard as to whether there was any sun shining at the time. That seemed to make no difference, so I at once put up my new black lace one much to Mamma's amusement." Clara was in a mood to find life amusing herself. She dined a good deal with the Lawrences and went shopping with Estelle. They thought the prices outrageous, and Clara wrote that the dressmakers were a perfect nuisance. "They promise things and do not even intend to give them when they have promised. I am perfectly tired out getting only three dresses. I have had nothing but bother over them." Even high spirits could not pardon such negligence.

During their stay in Paris, Mrs. Sears entered into her journal the words, "Belle and John called," indicating a visit from Isabella Stewart Gardner and her husband. Mrs. Sears and "Mrs. Jack" were related by marriage, in a complicated sort of way. Mrs. Sears' sister, Eliza, had married her cousin, George Augustus Gardner, who was the brother of Isabella's husband. As an art collector, "Mrs. Jack" was undoubtedly something of a model to Clara although their collections could not have been more different, Mrs. Gardner collecting European masters and Miss Sears early American primitives and the work of Hudson River School artists. Clara certainly did not emulate the flamboyance of Cousin Belle, but she did see in her a model for what a single-minded woman could achieve.

Clara may have been determined, but she was thoroughly conventional. Both she and her mother were too polite to tell Belle to her face what they thought of the recent and rather impressionistic portrait of her by Anders Zorn. Clara went to the

Salon du Champs de Mars to view it and could not abide it. When she returned to have a second look with Mamma a few days later, she was "again horrified," while Mrs. Sears called it a "horrid thing." Wealthy Bostonians customarily had their portraits painted while abroad, but nonrepresentational art was not for the Searses.

During a year's residence in Europe in 1878-1879, Clara and Mamie had sat for portraits by the French artist Leon Bonnat, and Clara later made a gift of Mamie's, "which Bonnat himself considered to be one of his best," to the Boston Museum of Fine Arts. On May 27, 1895, Mamma went to the studio of Emile Carolus Duran to speak to him about painting Clara. "I felt there was no chance but he consented. We go tomorrow morning at 9:30 for the first sitting." Although his style of painting was conventional, he was Bohemian in appearance and intrigued Clara much as Oscar Wilde had done. The portrait was completed in eight sittings, with Mamma and a student always in attendance. After the first sitting, Mrs. Sears wrote, "Promises well so far as the charcoal sketch goes." Other than that, she had little to note in her diary beyond the cost, 10,000 francs, and the fact that the artist rested by playing his guitar and singing French songs prettily.

After the May 31 sitting, Clara dined with the Lawrences and before going to bed was inspired to describe Monsieur Duran at length in her journal.

Unlike many artists Carolus Duran never speaks while painting and wishes his model to be absolutely quiet. But in the rests he knows how to make himself most charming in the easy natural way of the latin races. Yesterday when I was resting on the divan he went to the organ and played in a rambling dreamy but altogether delightful way - never saying much but going on as the mood took him. Then he came and sat in a chair - an old oak chair in which he looked like a Valasques picture with his gray hair and deep powerful eyes and brow. He always is most carefully dressed and wears a black velvet smoking jacket and sometimes a maroon colored one. As he sat there he took up his guitar and sang all sorts of lovely romantic songs in a sotto voce, smoking a cigarette between the verses. One I particularly took to was Le Chanson du Passanta by Massenet. It is most attractive. I made him sing it to me again in the afternoon. I notice, when he raises his sleeve in painting, that he wears a woman's bracelet on his left arm. His boots are patent leather and kept to perfection and his linen as white as snow. When he drew in my picture he did it with a new pair of pale yellow kid gloves on, so as not to soil his hands. This would have prejudiced me against him I think as being too much of a poseur, if I had not watched the masterly way he drew me on the canvas.

Mother and daughter were both pleased with the portrait. Wrote Clara, "As a likeness of me as seen in society, I think it excellent." Clearly implied in the statement was Clara's understanding of herself. She held a place in the society of wealthy Bostonians and wished to maintain it; she desired a place in the society of creative artists and had not yet found the means. Photography was only a hobby; she had long since discounted music; she lacked the drawing skills with which many of her family had been endowed; but she could write. Her journal was evidence of that. The amusing anecdotes were entered straight off, not labored over and later copied into it; and she was acquiring an ear for dialogue. Monsieur Duran was not a businessman and had become distressed when it was necessary to arrange for payment and shipment of the portrait. Miss Sears listened, remembered, and committed the conversation to her journal, in French.

On Tuesday, June 4, Clara and Mamma returned to England and a four-day rest at Highbury before taking the train to London, where Clara began a round of theater parties and excursions, mostly with the Lawrences. On June 11, Mrs. Sears noted, "Clara went to dine with the Lawrences at the Savoy Restaurant and to see Sarah Bernhardt afterwards." Clara wrote,

Estelle asked me to dine at the Savoy Restaurant and go to the theatre afterwards, so at seven o'clock I was arrayed in my new black satin low necked dress, and drove down there with Eliza the maid in a hansom. It was a lovely afternoon and I enjoyed the drive to the Savoy which is on the Thames Embankment. Hansoms were dashing in every direction with people in full dress inside of them on their way to dinners and entertainments. Jim ordered a very good dinner and took us to see Sarah Bernhardt act in "La Tosca." We had a box and I thoroughly enjoyed the whole thing. Everyone wears full evening dress at the theatres here so the scene is a brilliant one. Sarah Bernhardt acted superbly. She is a wonderful artist and every minute she was on the stage she acted her very best. She is wonderfully young looking for her age, which may be due to her make up, but whatever it is due to, she did not look a day over twenty-five. The play is a fearful tragedy. Tuesday, June 11, has become a special day.

The Divine's superb acting was but one aspect of Clara's special day. When in the company of the Lawrences, especially Jim, she found everything unusually delightful. Mrs. Sears' diary shows no sign of alarm, and Clara continued to chronicle events with the lightest of hearts. The young trio went off to Peterborough together, and when the old verger took them to tour the cathedral Clara found him "a perfectly killing person" and had difficulty in keeping a straight face. They spent the night at an inn, and Clara was given a room with two large beds and a cradle. She had a good sleep, "notwithstanding the extra empty bed and the cradle." At the time, at least, she thought a solitary slumber was what she would wish for the rest of her life.

There was one more memorable excursion before Mrs. Sears and the young people hired a carriage for Liverpool and took ship for New York. All four went to Hampton Court on a Sunday morning in mid June. At the maze Jim stood on a platform to watch the women, who became hopelessly confused. Clara opened her coquettish French parasol and led her mother in one direction while Estelle became lost in another. The man whose job it was to stand on a ladder and shout directions to those in need of them had to call out to Clara, "Will the little black umbrella please keep to the left!" Such was Clara's amusement that Mamma must have begun to suspect something was up whether Clara acknowledged it to herself or not.

By the 1900s, not only Clara and her mother but all Groton knew of her infatuation with Jim Lawrence. There is no knowing to what extent he reciprocated, but in any case divorce was unthinkable. There was severe social stigma attached to it, and there was also a powerful force against it right in Groton. The Reverend Endicott Peabody, founder of Groton School and Clara's cousin, was outspoken against divorce in general and adamant against it in particular. The next decade was the most difficult of Clara's life. From her thirties into her forties, she found herself as vulnerable as anyone else to the opposite sex. She clearly would have put Mamma second to a husband in the person of Jim Lawrence. She badly needed an outlet for her repressed emotions and became rather testy in everyday dealings. The domestic staff was careful to observe instructions to the letter, and the butcher made very sure that the loin lamb chops were cut to a full two-inch thickness.

Clara Sears had long been torn between her desire to conform and her desire to have her own way. In the matter of Jim Lawrence, she chose conformity and imposed on herself a control that she enforced by drawing increasingly on spiritual reserves. She read avidly from devotional literature, favoring the works of positive thinkers. She had no intention of sitting passively by, hoping some benign deity would diminish her frustration. Over the years she copied out helpful thoughts such as "Our mental attitude today determines our success tomorrow," and "Tranquillity is the outcome of decision, and we have the power to make our choice." The writings of contemporary clerics gave her solace as well as guidance. They became so essential to her well being that she compiled and printed *The Power Within*, a palm-sized volume of daily thoughts culled from the words of those who were guiding her toward a sustaining personal philosophy. In the foreword she wrote, "The thoughts this little book contains cannot fail to give poise to those who have lost their bearings; - a reasonable and well-founded joy to those who have become disheartened, and a law of living which makes even the rough places along the path seem worth while. This they have done for me. They will do it for you. I have never known them to fail."

Clara selected quotations that reflected the importance of self-knowledge and the healing powers of work. These were attributes that she acquired in abundance during the early 1900s and maintained for the rest of her life. They were the means by which she merged the spiritual and practical sides of her nature, the force by which she channeled her energy into the production of four museums, three novels, ten works of nonfiction, and a volume of poetry - all after age fifty.

In 1904, she and Mrs. Sears embarked on another trip to Europe, spending most of their time in Italy. Mamma hoped to bring her daughter out of the despondency she had fallen into, for no self-initiated change of circumstances had yet occurred to Clara. Mrs. Sears was the organizer this time, as well as the chronicler. Clara either wrote nothing or destroyed what she did write. Though she offered no insights into her daughter's state of mind, Mrs. Sears recorded enough information about external events to satisfy the most avid desire for detail. It was clearly her hope that Clara would fall in love with an attractive European nobleman, and her admiration for the high and the mighty was unmistakable. Clara had to submit to quite a grilling after one evening spent with ambassadors and Italian princes and princesses.

On the evening of April 21, 1904, Clara dined with the American ambassador in Rome, George Meyer, and his wife, Alice. Liveried servants stationed on the stairs ascending to the reception room announced arrivals. Mrs. Sears had made Clara promise to remember the august names since "all the company were of distinction and of diplomatic service and the opportunity was a rare one to meet so many beauties among the ladies and men of prominence in title and position." She felt the occasion to be "an open sesame" for her daughter. After the banquet, the party proceeded to a ball given by the Princess Terranova, who was first lady-in-waiting to the Queen of Italy. Whatever Clara's feelings, Mrs. Sears was impressed. Her daughter dutifully remembered all the royalty and near royalty, but when a "bevy of men" were presented to her during the dancing, it was too much for her overtaxed memory. She could not recall their names for Mamma.

The ball was of little significance to Clara; the highlight of her trip had already occurred. Two days earlier she and her mother had had an audience with Pope Pius X. The Searses were Episcopalians, but the Carney Hospital in Boston, to which Clara volunteered so much time, was a Roman Catholic institution. She had become very close to Sister Gonzaga there and wished the pope to bless a crucifix for the nun and the hospital. At the time, the pope was reluctant to give private audiences to Americans because several had refused to observe protocol in his presence. Thanks to the intervention of a Sears friend, Baron Schonberg, who was a chamberlain to the pope, Pius X agreed to make an exception.

Dressed in an accordion-pleated black dress of chiffon and wearing a black veil, a nervous Clara engaged a carriage and drove to the Vatican in the company of her mother and the Baron and Baroness Schonberg. Two cardinals led them through various public and private chambers, creating quite a stir among waiting Roman matrons, velvet clad and pearl bejewelled, who whispered at their presence. Clara, to her relief, curtsied faultlessly upon presentation to the pope and then went forward to kneel for his blessing and to kiss the enormous diamond and emerald pontifical ring. His Holiness, in white robes of heavily corded silk, was "a very tall, imposing man of strong and reverend bearing," and she was unable to imagine the disrespect shown by some of her countrymen. Baroness Schonberg, more agitated than the others by the pope's special favor, translated his words into English as he blessed the crucifix and thanked Clara for her good works. The pope personally raised Mrs. Sears from her knees and smiled kindly as they all backed from his presence and performed a final curtsy. Not only were they very much moved by the audience, they were also "well fatigued."

In 1906, Clara took one more trip to Europe, again with her mother, and as each successive spring approached she became more reluctant to return to Groton. She felt constrained there, too much reined in by resident and visiting Peabodys, who were ever observant of her behavior and demanding of her time. She claimed that Groton was altogether too social and meant it. There was always something doing, and she preferred to be less thrown into the society of the Lawrences; she wanted to enjoy the country in peace. Miss Sears came to the conclusion that she would have to move elsewhere. Her mother was in her early seventies and willing to have Clara take charge of one of their households. There were now only two since they visited Nahant less and less. The estate that replaced Riverdale Farm would be their home from early spring to late autumn, and Miss Sears could incorporate into it a working farm under her direct and continuous supervision. Work was becoming her sustaining force, and her insistence on taking matters into her own hands was becoming well known. The *Boston Transcript* reported her proposed move, setting the tone of future press comments. "When Clara Endicott Sears decided to sell her estate in Groton, she had a sign placed in front of the house. It announced 'This Place For Sale. Inquire Within.' A simple and direct statement, such as this lady always makes. Those who knew her realized that it is the unexpected thing she does and they will probably agree that she personally selected the tree on which the sign was fastened and, possibly, put in the nails herself."

In the nearby town of Harvard was a ridge called Prospect Hill, once known by the Nashaway Indians as Makamacheckamucks. Its western view of Mt. Wachusett and the mountains of southern New Hampshire was much like that of Riverdale Farm, but even more spectacular. Clara Sears purchased thirty-eight acres there in 1910 and added several hundred more over the next few years. The move succeeded in bringing long-sought tranquillity of mind but not peace and quiet. First came the flurry of building; then a fortuitous discovery that began her career as a preservationist.

Miss Sears designed the house in Harvard herself and called it "a villa with English comforts." Although inclined to be a bit close with her inherited wealth, she made no concessions to cost and brooked no criticism of her plans. She decided to use for her own the elegant doorway that had once graced the entrance to Great-grandfather Joseph Peabody's Salem mansion. There were those who suggested that its balcony and iron grillwork were too ornate, but she insisted on having her own way. As she told a reporter for the *Worcester Gazette*, "If a place is to speak of its owner, no alien taste should come into it." The doorway was installed, and the white clapboard country home was enhanced not only by ironwork but also by ancient Venetian stonework that Miss Sears had purchased during her 1906 trip to Venice. Everyone had to agree that the whole was a most agreeable composite.

Wealthy Bostonians at that time frequently imported objects of Italian marble for their Back Bay homes and Newport cottages. When Isabella Stewart Gardner opened Fenway Court in 1903, guests looked down on her flower-filled inner courtyard from no less than eight Venetian balconies. Miss Sears was merely following precedent in purchasing elaborate wellheads and heavily carved Byzantine columns. The columns had formed an arbor, or pergola, in the gardens of an ancient monastery that was being demolished. Miss Sears set them similarly and named her estate the Pergolas. Where the earth of her hillside slanted downward toward the valley of the Nashua River, she built a terrace and circled it with marble columns, many of which were surmounted by huge stone eagles. She instructed her gardeners to place great pots of colorful flowers about the terrace and to position stone benches so that she might enjoy a quiet moment from time to time. The distant mountains represented strength to her. She felt an intimacy with nature as she watched their changing aspect, and she began to write the poetry which was her essential emotional outlet.

Miss Sears had not owned her initial thirty-eight acres long when she discovered that the adjacent property had been the scene of Bronson Alcott's 1843 experiment in communal living. She immediately purchased the land and his Fruitlands farm-house and plunged into the work of its restoration. Though his-toric preservation was uncommon at the time, it was not without precedent for Miss Sears, whose circle included members of the Massachusetts Historical Society and the Society for the Preserva-tion of New England Antiquities. She became so involved in her projects as to forestall family criticism when she adopted a social schedule of luncheons only.

It was by her own choice that Clara Sears had no close friends. She regretted seeing so little of Cousin Mary, but there was no helping it; and Cousin Fanny was almost as busy as Clara. New associations evolved and were initially connected with her research. Frank Sanborn, who had known Bronson Alcott personally and was his first biographer, lived in nearby Concord. Sanborn helped Miss Sears greatly with both information and artifacts, and he and his wife were frequent guests at her lun-cheons. After one such occasion Mrs. Sanborn responded with an effusive note typical of the style of the era. "I feel as if I had made a visit to Fairy Land and brought home the sweetest memo-ries of it - Heaven gave us the most beautiful Day of Days, and your graceful hospitality did the rest...." Such notes pleased Miss Sears no end, by showing that she was as much a social success as ever. However, she arranged these new personal relationships to suit her convenience and did not expend emotional energy upon them. That she saved for her writing.

With so much going on, she had little time for writing. On the rare occasions when she found a spare moment during the day, she wrote in the seclusion of a Venetian cloister that she had built against the retaining wall of her hillside home. Marble busts of ancient philosophers lined its length, and her favorite spot was a corner where she installed sculptured heads of Alcott, Emerson, Thoreau, and Hawthorne. In thanking Miss Sears for a photograph she had taken of the Pergolas, Frank Sanborn pleased her when he mused, "It would have delighted Alcott to have Venice thus transferred to Fruitlands." As she came to know more and more about that American mystic, Miss Sears felt it to be true.

Governor John Winthrop
1587-1649

Governor John Endicott
1588-1665

Joseph Peabody
1757-1844

Clarissa Endicott Peabody
1806-1892

George Peabody
1804-1892

David Sears, the Younger
1787-1871

Knyvet Winthrop Sears
1832-1891

Mary Peabody Sears
1836-1929

The George Peabody Mansion, Washington Square, Salem

The Peabodys' large drawing room, designed by Lamonier

The Farm (Glen Magna), Danvers

Summer home in Nahant

Southward portrait
of Clara Sears
1870

Clara Sears, London
1895

Mary Endicott
age 15

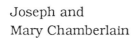

Joseph and
Mary Chamberlain

Clara Sears, 1912

The Pergolas

Miss Sears' cloister

View from her terrace

The Pergolas, interior view

Fruitlands Farmhouse, 1914, as it appeared
when first opened to the public

Clara Sears and Shakers in front of
Fruitlands, about 1916

Eldress Josephine Jilson

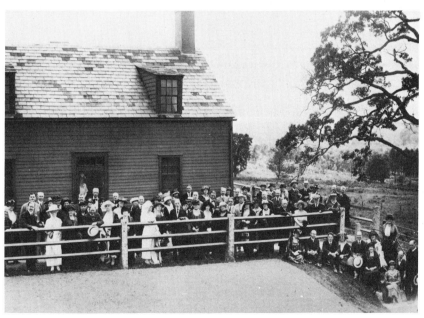

Dedication of the Shaker Museum, 1922

The author Sara Ware Bassett
with Clara Sears

Clara Sears, 1917

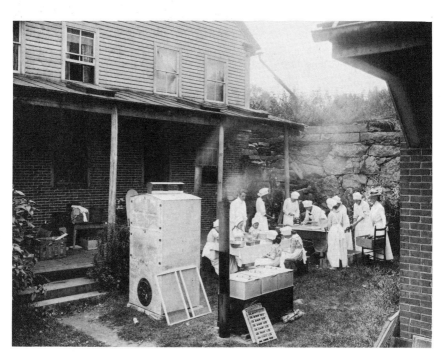

The Canning and Evaporating Club

Unveiling of *Pumunangwet*, 1931.
Miss Sears with Chief Buffalo Bear
and with the sculptor, her cousin
Philip Sears

Miss Sears,
Philip Sears,
and Indian guests at
the unveiling of
the *Dreamer*, 1938

Miriam Shaw, Mrs. Sears,
Clara Sears

Miss Sears in her portrait gallery with paintings
by Chester Harding and Francis Alexander

Portrait of Clara Endicott Sears
by Alfred Jonniaux, 1949

CHAPTER 5

A New Eden

*When I think of the study, thought, and
intelligence you have put into it all,
I am lost in admiration. I cannot imagine
any restoration better done than yours.*

William Endicott, President
Society for the Preservation
of New England Antiquities

Glen Magna was not the only farm in Clara Sears' background, although it was the one with which she was most familiar. Governor John Endicott had been granted Orchard Farm, "a necke of land lyeing aboute 3 myles from Salem, cont aboute 300 ac of land, ...to enioy to him and his heires for ever...." It was here that Clara's great-uncle William used to go blueberrying with his older sisters, who "told him that blueberries tasted much better if eaten on a pin, while they, themselves, ate them by the handful." It was here that the famous pear tree continued to bear even beyond the Honorable William Endicott's tenure in Washington.

Clara Sears did not limit herself to building a fine country home when she bought her estate in the town of Harvard; she fulfilled her long-held ambition to establish a farm, and she hired a resident farmer to live just down the road. Few children gathered either memories or fruit at the Pergolas, for it was strictly an adult establishment. In truth, Miss Sears preferred the notion of childhood to children themselves and did not mind the lack. For her part, she no longer had to wait for spring picnics at The Farm in order to take a look at the cows. She knew the health of all her animals, and in her Line-A-Day notebook she recorded production figures, calvings, and the auctions at which she bought and sold livestock. Nor was she too much the lady to record her ire when she discovered that her farmer had been allowing a neighbor to "bring his cows to be served by my bull." So that she could keep tabs on all that was happening year-round, her chauffeur drove her from 132 Beacon Street to Harvard at least once a week during winter months. She had the wealth to serve her ends, used it for her convenience, and had the reputation of a patrician who did things herself.

The ever-interested press continued to follow her doings. Written about anyone else, the following article in the *Boston American* must surely have been tongue-in-cheek; but whether exaggerating or not, reporters were always respectful of Miss Sears, almost in awe of this many-faceted woman. The word "aristocratic" appeared again and again, and it is not altogether surprising to see it applied to her livestock.

> Miss Sears knows exactly when each calf is born, she herself registers each animal on the place, she buys every single seed planted in the large vegetable and flower garden, and she can tell you precisely how many cans of milk and cream are shipped to Boston to be sold.
>
> There are over 400 acres to the farm. The fifty-odd registered Guernsey cattle have all been raised on the place. They are very aristocratic bovines and give such pure milk

that it's all bought by Boston physicians. There are farm horses and more than half a dozen dogs, of which Miss Sears is especially fond.

Miss Sears had a finely honed sense of her place in the social scale, but liked to think of herself as a friend to those in the more common walks of life, and so she was, as long as liberties were not taken. Hence she could refer to her "friend," a seamstress who asked for advice about using her savings to buy a farm. Miss Sears urged her to do so, saying "If a woman is really willing to work she will find farm life fascinating." Although she, of course, did not do the physical labor, Miss Sears worked hard at making her own farm a success. It took years to achieve the perfection that brought her blue ribbons and local respect.

When she purchased her original acreage, Miss Sears had no knowledge of its historical significance. The dilapidated old farmhouse at the bottom of the hill offended her sense of the aesthetic, and at first she wished to own it simply in order to correct an eyesore; ultimately, it was the catalyst that began her professional life. The restoration of the Fruitlands farmhouse launched her career as a preservationist; the compilation of relevant documents, letters, and diaries established her as an author of stature. With Houghton Mifflin's publication of her *Bronson Alcott's Fruitlands* in 1915, she began the intellectual life for which her background had prepared her.

There was a Shaker village in the town of Harvard, and the transcendentalists had been much attracted by Shaker philosophy, visiting frequently with the elders there. During the course of her research, Miss Sears became friendly with the eldresses. The two influences, transcendental and Shaker, led her receptive mind beyond the spiritual life she already embraced, and she came to believe in mystical communion. She claimed to feel Alcott's presence while restoring his dwelling, cultivating the acres of his New Eden, and chronicling his lost utopia. Where the impractical transcendentalists failed, however, Miss Sears succeeded. Though a budding mystic, she was no dreamer. Her hard work in restoring his farmhouse as a museum and in writing the story of his eight months in Harvard gave a measure of substance to Alcott's idealism.

Miss Sears begins her introduction to *Bronson Alcott's Fruitlands* with some lines of Henry Wadsworth Longfellow.

> All houses wherein men have lived and died
> Are haunted houses. Through the open doors
> The harmless phantoms on their errands glide,
> With feet that make no sound upon the floors.
>
> We meet them at the doorway, on the stair,
> Along the passages they come and go,
> Impalpable impressions on the air,
> A sense of something moving to and fro.

The poem expresses feelings akin to those which had always moved her profoundly when in the presence of history, and she found herself reciting the lines whenever her eyes rested upon the old house of Fruitlands. In the introduction to *Bronson Alcott's Fruitlands*, Clara Sears sets forth portions of her personal philosophy, providing a sort of spiritual autobiography. Her style and outlook are clearly romantic, but her sense of the need to honor and remember history dominates her mysticism and prevents it from getting out of hand. She clearly knows that her place in the scheme of things is to preserve and document.

> From my terrace on the hill I looked down upon it with mixed feelings of pity, awe, and affection. It seemed like a Presence, a ghost of the Past, that compelled the eyes to gaze at it persistently. In the warm joyousness of the spring sunshine, or when the cold mists of autumn crept across the valley, it conveyed to me the same sense of desolation, of mystery, of disillusionment. Its broken windows looked like hollow eyes sunken in an ashen and expressionless face. Within its walls life and death had come and gone; - laughter and the sound of weeping had echoed through the quaint, low-ceilinged rooms....

But it was when the old house had begun to settle and look decrepit, and its floors had become shaky and uneven, that its door opened wide to its supreme experience. Then Fruitlands was exalted into the New Eden. The two names came to it simultaneously. It was to pulsate with lofty ideals and altruistic aspirations. For one perfect summer and mellow autumn its running brook, its shady grove, its fertile meadows and sloping pasture, its western view, so beautiful at sundown, of Wachusett and Monadnoc, and the chain of purple hills, were to be the inspiration of a group of individuals then known as the transcendental philosophers, and through them Fruitlands became famous....

So as I looked down on it from my terrace on the hill, pitying its infinite loneliness, the thought came to me that I must save it. If for a time it had borne the semblance of a New Eden, then that time must be honored, and not forgotten. I longed to see it smiling again upon the valley in its glowing coat of ochre-red. The fine old chimneys must be put back in their places from which they had been ruthlessly torn down to make room for stoves. The hollow eyes must gleam again with window-panes; the sound of voices must ring once more through the empty rooms. In the future it must be cherished for its quaintly interesting history. If that history was full of pathos, if the great experiment enacted beneath its roof proved a failure, the failure was only in the means of expression and not in the ideal which inspired it. Humanity must ever reach out towards a New Eden. Succeeding generations smile at the crude attempts, and forthwith make their own blunders, but each attempt, however seemingly unsuccessful, must of necessity contain a germ of spiritual beauty which will bear fruit. Let no one cross the threshold of the old house with a mocking heart. Looking back from our present coigne of vantage, we, too, cannot but smile at the childlike simplicity and credulity, and the lack of forethought of those unpractical enthusiasts. But let it be the smile of tenderness and not of derision. In this material age we cannot afford to lose any details of so unique and picturesque a memory as that of A. Bronson Alcott and the Con-Sociate Family at Fruitlands.

Miss Sears drew inspiration from the same exquisite view described by Messrs. Alcott and Lane in the transcendentalist *Dial* of July 1843.

> For picturesque beauty both in the near and the distant landscape, the spot has few rivals. A semi-circle of undulating hills stretches from south to west, among which the Wachusett and Monadnoc are conspicuous. The vale, through which flows a tributary to the Nashua, is esteemed for its fertility and ease of cultivation, is adorned with groves of nut-trees, maples, and pines, and watered by small streams. Distant not thirty miles from the metropolis of New England, this reserve lies in a serene and sequestered dell. No public thoroughfare invades it, but it is entered by a private road. The nearest hamlet is that of Stillriver [sic], a field's walk of twenty minutes, and the village of Harvard is reached by circuitous and hilly roads of nearly three miles.

It was here that these idealists planned to form a family in the communal sense, to number ten or so adults, as well as the four Alcott daughters and Charles Lane's son. They would minimize creature comforts while consecrating their souls to unselfish, and unspecified, spiritual uses. The kingdom of peace could be entered "only through the gates of self-denial," and redemption was contingent upon simplification of life. "Ordinary secular farming" was not their object. Since innocent sheep were not to be deprived of their wool nor cows of their milk, the con-sociate family dressed in homespun and drank cooling well water. Since they intended "to supersede...the labor of the plough and cattle by the spade and the pruning knife," they planned to liberate oxen from their tasks until, as Louisa May Alcott expressed it later in a gentle parody of the experience, there remained only one beast of burden on the property, Mrs. Alcott.

At first all went well. The Alcott girls readily accepted their father's wisdom as shown in a composition by twelve-year-old Anna.

Life was given to the animals not to be destroyed by men, but to make them happy, and that they might enjoy life. But men are not satisfied with slaying the innocent creatures, but they eat them and so make their bodies of flesh meat. O how many lives have been destroyed and how many loving families have been separated to please an unclean appetite of men! Why were the fruits, berries and vegetables given us if it was intended that we should eat flesh? I am sure it was not. We enjoy the beautiful sights and thoughts God has given us in peace. Why not let them do the same? We have souls to feel and think with, and as they have not the same power of thinking, they should be allowed to live in peace and not made to labour so hard and be beaten so much. Then to eat them!.... If treated kindly, they would be kind and tame and love men, but as they now are abused and cruelly treated they do not feel the feeling of "love" towards men. Besides flesh is not clean food, and when there is beautiful juicy fruits who can be a flesh-eater?

The productivity of Miss Sears' herd might have convinced these transcendentalists that she treated her innocent animals kindly and did them a service by relieving them of their milky burden. The Harvard newspaper reported some statistics under the heading Production Record.

Miss C.E. Sears of this town has recently won national recognition on her pure bred Guernsey bull, Meredith Gladiator 113864. This bull, having two daughters which have made creditable official records, has been entered in the advanced register of the American Guernsey Cattle club, and will be known hereafter as an advanced register sire. Only Guernseys which meet high production requirements are eligible for entry.... A cow in the herd of Miss Sears has just finished a new official record for production which entitles her to entry in the advanced register of the American Guernsey Cattle club. This animal is a four-year-old, Nashua Sunburst 220865 with a production of 10,816.4 pounds of milk and 595.2 pounds of fat in Class C.

The names of Miss Sears' cows were often prefaced with the name of the nearby intervale, as in Nashua Merry Lass, Nashua Moonlight. In the early summer of 1843, Anna Alcott, who was to become the Meg of *Little Women*, praised the idyllic beauty of the spot, admiring the mountains beyond the valley of the Nashua River and enjoying pleasant walks about Fruitlands "though the berries were not yet quite ripe." She found it a pleasant place to live.

By fall, however, the girls had lost their enthusiasm for cold showers at dawn, bread and fruit for dinner, and questions of philosophy. Ten-year-old Louisa May made this entry in her journal and annotated it in adulthood.

> Anna and I did the work. In the evening Mr. Lane asked us, "What is man?" These were our answers: A human being; an animal with a mind; a creature; a body; a soul and a mind. After a long talk we went to bed very tired.
>
> (No wonder, after doing the work and worrying their little wits with such lessons. - L.M.A.)

By winter, discontent had given way to disillusionment, hunger was a serious threat, and Charles Lane was urging Bronson Alcott to forsake his family for the celibate community of nearby Shakers. Louisa May's entry for December 10 was one of despair.

> I did my lessons, and walked in the afternoon. Father read to us in dear "Pilgrim's Progress." Mr. L. was in Boston and we were glad. In the eve father and mother and Anna and I had a long talk. I was very unhappy, and we all cried. Anna and I cried in bed, and I prayed God to keep us all together.

The philosophers had sited their fruit trees disadvantageously, had plowed under edible crops for fertilizer in place of animal manures, and had neglected what harvest there might have been. Scant supplies diminished to the point that kindly neighbors offered first sustenance and finally shelter. The Fruitlands experiment had come to an end.

Clara Sears and Bronson Alcott dreamed dreams and shared common soil. Miss Sears felt that the essence of utopian endeavors existed in their attempt, not necessarily in their success. As she put it, Alcott's failure "was only in the means of expression and not in the ideal which inspired it." She became intrigued with the question of whether Alcott felt he had gained from his attempts, albeit unsuccessful, to find moral and mental stimulation in the purity of physical labor. She herself was certainly the richer for the intellectual impetus given her by Alcott's experiment. Alcott once told Anna that if a person wanted a thing very much and thought of it a great deal, he would probably have it. With Clara Sears, thought was invariably followed by action. She brought about her independence by the purchase of land in Harvard and then involved herself totally in planning and overseeing construction of the Pergolas. At mid-life, with the discovery of the con-sociate family's dwelling, she immersed herself in the scholarly work which had so long eluded her.

Miss Sears was as indefatigable in her pursuit of artifacts for the farmhouse restoration as in her research for *Bronson Alcott's Fruitlands.* She took great pains to relocate furnishings that had been removed and, in so doing, involved herself personally with many heirs of the original Harvard transcendentalists. One of the more practical of the original group, bearded patriarch Joseph Palmer, purchased the Fruitlands property after the departures of Lane and Alcott, and one of his grandsons was born in the old farmhouse. This grandson told Miss Sears stories of his boyhood and helped her immeasurably. Joseph Palmer had been a sensible farmer and introduced a yoke and team onto the premises when the idealistic transcendentalists finally admitted that they could not dig enough earth with spades alone. Miss Sears displayed this yoke at her museum in the spirit of historical interest, not of derision.

In Concord, Miss Sears found that Alcott heirs were delighted with her project and glad to give her as much help as they were able. She often took tea with Jessica Pratt, whose deceased husband was Anna Alcott's son, Frederick Alcott Pratt. In accordance with an old family tradition, Mrs. Pratt kept Alcott treasures in a box under the bed and generously parted with many of them for both Fruitlands and Orchard House, the Alcott museum in Concord. After Miss Sears' acknowledgment of one such gift, Mrs. Pratt replied on May 23, 1915,

> I am glad the little relics filled their places so acceptably at Fruitlands. It is indeed a satisfaction and pleasure to find some one who really understands the spirit of those days, and cares so much for these pathetic souvenirs of the pathetic episode so bravely undertaken, and so wholly lived through even to the bitter end.... So it seems almost a sacred obligation, as well as pleasure, that in some small measure even, I can help by placing these simple remembrances at Fruitlands....
>
> I am sending the lock of hair I promised - as I found it - as it was left - with Miss Alcott's own initials and handwriting, - I have some of Mrs. Pratt's but think none is left of the others....
>
> I was very glad to see you a fortnight or more ago, and hear more fully of your ideas and plans in connection with the wonderful labour of love you have carried out at Fruitlands. Perhaps you will come again some time, if you have the interest and leisure to look into some of the Diaries and letters.

Jessica Pratt's brother-in-law, John, also gave generously of time and advice. He had been legally adopted by Louisa May Alcott in 1888, becoming John Pratt Alcott, somewhat to the confusion of *Little Women* devotees who knew perfectly well that there were four Alcott daughters and no sons who could carry on the family name. In reply to a letter from Miss Sears on Fruitlands matters, John Pratt Alcott offered a caustic comment on the family shrine in Concord.

74

I am sorry to hear that Orchard House did not make a better showing this season. I think that next Summer I shall have to go out there and sell Alcott books to the visitors, a sort of remnant sale, the Alcott books sold by a human Alcott remnant, don't you think it would make a hit.

On June 20, 1914, Miss Sears opened her museum at Fruit-lands and held the first of what she came to call her museum luncheons, catered affairs that were always meticulously staged. The spontaneity of her twenties and thirties had given way to a total seriousness of purpose. On this occasion, there was no cos-tumed piece of theater as in future openings, but the Salem Cadet orchestra "rendered choice music" while she received her guests out of doors. This June entertainment was a mere warm-up for lavish luncheons to come. In October of the same year, she entertained the managers of the Society for the Preservation of New England Antiquities. Although a number of guests came in their own automobiles, most traveled by the 11:15 train from Boston and were met by a bus Miss Sears chartered for the occa-sion. Before viewing the museum, the company dined upon con-sommé, quenelles, scalloped oysters, chicken croquettes, French peas, duck à la voisin, Russian salad, gateaux, and ices.

Miss Sears, so capable, so forthright in her manner, so assured to all outward appearances, lacked much of the confi-dence attributed to her. She needed assurances in regard to both her work and her parties, the grown-up equivalent of the "wasn't she wise" that followed her childhood triumphs. Fortunately, men and women of her circle were accustomed to writing one another frequently; admiration and respect were openly and freely bestowed upon her and her efforts. For the rest of her life she kept such letters in labeled volumes. In part, Clara Sears was playing a role at her luncheons, aware of the impressions she wished to create and eager for the resulting applause. Though she saw to her guests' comfort with genuine warmth, she became more and more exacting in the requirements of her productions. In 1916, a printed card was enclosed with the seventy invitations to a festivity for the Colonial Dames.

> As there will be a great many motors at the luncheon for the Colonial Dames given by Miss Sears at Harvard, Massachusetts, on Tuesday, June 6, at one o'clock, will you kindly give the following instructions to your chauffeur:
> Upon arriving at Miss Sears' please go back over the road to Harvard Village to The Harvard Woman's Club Exchange and Tea Room.
> The sign is on the steps outside. Lunch will be served there.
> Be back at Miss Sears' at 2 p.m. and wait in the road in single file ready to go on to Fruitlands.

By the 1930s, with the addition of the Indian Museum, her openings had evolved into a pageantry that rivaled that of Isabella Stewart Gardner's 1903 flower- and music-filled extravaganza at Fenway Court. While Will Dodge's luncheon music was hardly equal to that of the Boston Symphony Orchestra, which played for Mrs. Gardner, the authentic Indian dancing which took place in front of the new museum was sufficiently spectacular. So precisely did Miss Sears time the proceedings and so rigid had she become that she felt she had to dispatch the following memo prior to the occasion:

> My chauffeur (Sharples) is to go to Boston to get three persons. He will then go to the Copley-Plaza and lead the way up here, - but I do not want the people in the Bus to know this, for they might want to get into the car, and three is all it can hold comfortably. I do this so as to be sure of the punctual arrival of the Bus. It appears that the last time the people in the Bus told the driver that he had taken the wrong turn, and showed him the card of directions, but he would not pay any attention to them and said he was going his own way! There is too much involved this time to run any risk. At the same time I want a man who knows the way thoroughly in case anything happened to prevent Sharples from going there. I enclose some cards.

> As I said the Bus would leave the Copley-Plaza at 11:30 a.m. I think people should get there in time, and on this occasion I cannot have the start delayed. Five minutes grace is all we can undertake to allow. Of course we must have the musicians, but I have written to Mr. Dodge that they must be sure to be on time. I do hope that all will go right, and I think it will. The big card with Private Bus on it is at 132 Beacon St., on the table near the front door.

Her demand for perfection had made her brusque in commonplace dealings but she always personified graciousness in her entertainments, and invitations to her luncheons were much coveted. The assurances she required poured in, and the contents of her bound volumes grew apace. Luncheons had the advantage of permitting Miss Sears to remain socially involved while retaining the freedom to write in the evenings. Moreover, they produced the praise she so needed. Guests' thank-you notes enthusiastically attested to their pleasure in being with her and in visiting her museums, and she finally began to relax and enjoy their admiring faces while, as she phrased it, "the view and the surroundings [took] their breath away."

Mrs. Sears encouraged Clara in her work, shared in her triumphs, attended all the luncheons, and was much mentioned in notes of appreciation. Among the guests at the Pergolas were her cousins and friends of long standing, the Loring sisters. Louise, head of the Massachusetts Red Cross, wrote Clara,

> Yesterday was a memorable day for my happiness! for my admiration! How can I thank you enough for what you gave to us.... To have made a poem of your page of history in that beautiful New England surrounding is surely an event of a life time.... It was such a crowning pleasure to be with Cousin Mary again!

Katharine Loring, long-time companion to the invalid Alice James, contributed two anecdotes about the days when Bronson Alcott and Ralph Waldo Emerson were neighbors in Concord.

Dear Clara,

Probably you have heard these stories of Mr. Alcott, but in case you have not:

Mr. Alcott and Mr. Emerson would stand talking over the fence in the mornings. Mr. A. would not say anything but listened to Mr. Emerson, and in the afternoon he would repeat as his own whatever Mr. Emerson told him: and Mr. Emerson would go home and say, "how wise Alcott is!"

The other story, the two sages were talking across the garden fence and Mr. Emerson said, "how is it my potatoes are covered with bugs and yours haven't any?" "Well," said Mr. Alcott, "the fault is I catch bugs all the morning, but as I cannot bear to take life, I just throw them over into your field!"

If these are chestnuts forgive me.

Give my love to Cousin Molly and believe me

Yours affectionately,

Katharine P. Loring

Both philosophers had been personal friends of "the last sage of Concord," Frank Sanborn, who spoke at the opening of Miss Sears' Fruitlands Museum and contributed valuable critical comments as she compiled material for *Bronson Alcott's Fruitlands*. Its publication brought forth favorable national reviews and supplied a welcome boost to help alleviate her self-doubts. The *New York Times* devoted the front page of its "Sunday Book Review" to the volume, acknowledging the scholarship Miss Sears manifested, "having devoted herself with the utmost patience to digging up all the records available."

When Odell Shepard published his book on Alcott, *Pedlar's Progress*, twenty-two years later, he paid his older colleague a compliment in his text. "The story of outward events at Fruitlands has already been told with such accuracy and sympathetic justice by another pen (that of Clara Endicott Sears) that a brief outline of them may here suffice."

Miss Sears had unwillingly concluded that Alcott, in despair over his failure at Fruitlands, must have destroyed his journals for the years 1842-1844. The assumption was not unreasonable inasmuch as neither she nor Frank Sanborn had been able to discover them. Nevertheless, she continued to feel that such an act of destruction was incompatible with Alcott's own statement that he had grown as a result of the experiment. During the course of his subsequent research, Odell Shepard consulted frequently with Miss Sears and agreed with her on this point. They were both reassured when Mr. Shepard found further evidence in Alcott's journal of 1869.

> But I can hardly conceive anything more conducive to my spiritual advantage than the experiences of those years at Fruitlands and return to Concord. I think I may say that my defeats have proved victories. I did not plant the Paradise geographically as I fancied I might but entered spiritually into a fairer Eden than I sought to people with human kind.

Finally, in a letter dated August 29, 1935, Shepard was able to inform Miss Sears of a newly discovered note, in Alcott's own hand, that established without a doubt that he had lost the journals while on a trip to Albany. This proof of Alcott's loyalty to his dream resolved the doubts she had harbored for twenty years and rewarded her for her continuing intellectual involvement with the matter.

John Pratt Alcott also held generous thoughts toward his impractical grandfather. In his foreword to *Bronson Alcott's Fruitlands* he complimented Miss Sears on writing "the first connected story of the life and beliefs of that little community which tried so hard to live according to its ideals in spite of criticism and censure...." He also wrote to her privately.

> I feel that in publishing the "Fruitlands" you have placed the family under a debt which they can never repay and I wish to thank you once more, both personally and as the

Head of the family for what you have done and for the beautiful method you have taken to perpetuate the memory of that wonderful though unpractical and ill-fated attempt at the ideal (to them) community life.

As a result of her book, Clara Endicott Sears was awarded recognition she particularly coveted, membership in the Boston Authors' Club. Naturally, she celebrated with a luncheon. On June 14, 1916, seventy-five club members arrived for their first annual luncheon at the Pergolas. Letter after letter congratulated her personally and professionally and also acknowledged Mrs. Sears' devotion to her daughter's efforts. Charles E. Mann summed it up.

> Take the word of an expert editor, who read [Bronson Alcott's Fruitlands] with discretion as well as delight, that your work of compilation has been so carefully and wisely - as well as thoroughly - done as to make the words you have quoted your own....
>
> I had not supposed that such a lovely prospect of valley and mountains existed anywhere in Massachusetts, and I do not wonder that 10 year old Louisa May Alcott, going up on the hill before breakfast "had some thoughts - it was so beautiful." It added so much to our happiness to see it all in the surroundings of your beautiful home and to be recipients of the unremitting attentions of your mother and yourself.

For the rest of her life, the Authors' Club played a dominant role in Clara Sears' activities. It was from this group that she formed friendships with Alice Brown, Emilie Loring, and Sara Ware Bassett. She attended the group's Boston meetings faithfully; and each summer she entertained its members, secure at last in the acceptance of her intellectual peers. Judge Robert Grant, who wrote "The Fatal Sisters" in admiration of Clara and Mamie in 1882, had become prominent in both law and literature and was a loyal member of the group. He and his wife were in regular attendance, and at one Pergolas luncheon he gave a eulogy that tested Miss Clara's self-control, as she acknowledged in her account of the occasion to her trustees.

Then Judge Grant arose and spoke for the Club in appreciation of my work, literary and otherwise. I was perfectly overcome by all that he said. He was quite emotional at one part, and so of course that made me feel so too, but fortunately we did not make a scene!

When the day came to an end and they drove off waving their hands and their hats and their handkerchiefs at me I felt that it was indeed a Red letter day for me.

Chapter 6

Hands to Work

*The only really successful extensive Community
of interest, spiritual and secular, in modern
times was established by A Woman.*
Charles Lane and Bronson Alcott

It was inevitable that Clara Sears introduce herself to the Harvard Shakers during the course of her research on the Fruit-lands transcendentalists. Miss Sears, Eldress Josephine Jilson, and Eldress Annie Walker hit it off from the start, strong spinster women that they all were. Miss Sears found the Shaker motto, "Give your hands to work and your hearts to God," reminiscent of her grandmother Peabody's maxim, "Give out something from within." The three women were doers, though Miss Sears was of the world and the eldresses were restricted to the confines of the Shaker society.

The Shaker sect was founded by Mother Ann Lee, who arrived from England in 1774 with eight followers, all Shaking Quakers, in search of freedom to practice a religious blend of mysticism and practicality. Persecution and stonings followed the establishment of early Shaker settlements in New York, Connecticut, and Massachusetts; and mobs in Harvard manifested the particular ferocity associated with fear of the unfamiliar. In the eyes of the world, the strange ecstasies of Shaker religious fervor overshadowed the utilitarian excellence of their craftsmanship and husbandry although, by the time Miss Sears came to know the Harvard Shakers, the excesses of shaking and whirling had abated, replaced by more sober images. In their gray dresses, white caps and kerchiefs, Eldresses Annie and Josephine were the essence of decorum as they sipped tea while enjoying the view from Miss Sears' terrace or as they sat in their own rocking chairs, chatting about earlier days.

Miss Sears was eager to learn all she could about the background of the Harvard Shaker Village. Through the aging eldresses she was able to envision the scenes of long-ago times when, as she wrote in *Gleanings from Old Shaker Journals*, "a farmer going down a country road at dusk was liable to see two or more figures spinning like tops along the side of the road, so fast that in their gray clothes they looked like winged insects that whirl through the air along the swamps and damp places, especially towards nightfall. Of course the sight of this to the farmer's mind had something to do with the devil, and he would turn his horse around and make for his home as fast as he could."

Miss Sears personally observed evidence of the lingering superstitions of Harvard townspeople. She suffered for the sisters, who were on occasion still troubled by irrational accusations.

I well remember going into a little shop in the Shaker Village one day where they sold homemade peppermints, and apple sauce, and fancy pincushions, and such things characteristic of the Shakers, and seeing a young woman standing by the counter buying peppermints for her little girl who was standing beside her. Eldress Annie Walker was Head Eldress at the time, and she came round the counter. "Thee is a sweet child," she said to the little girl, and she put her hand on her shoulder. The mother uttered a scream. "Don't do that!" she cried. "Don't do that! Take your hand off my child's shoulder!" And turning to me she said in a trembling undertone, "She might bewitch the child! Who knows?"

Clara Sears felt compassion for the eldresses, who were stoic but saddened by such incidents, and she admired the serenity with which they managed to carry on. Shakers no longer let it be known that there were those among them who still heard spirit voices, but Miss Sears saw a great deal of them and, as she said, "It was impossible to be with them and not to become imbued more or less with their state of mind. And strange things happened there." Twenty-five years after the event, she told the tale which convinced her it was possible to communicate with the other world.

Miss Sears was driven over to Shaker Village one day, to pick up some old chairs that were being recaned under Eldress Josephine's supervision. An eldress who was standing near the stone steps leading to the office building made no response to Miss Sears' cheery greeting, so she repeated her "Good afternoon" but still received no answer. Wondering very much about the reason for this lack of cordiality, Miss Sears called out, "Aren't you going to speak to me, what is the matter?" Not only was there still no response, but the eldress turned her back, ascended the stone steps, and entered the building. In telling of the experience, Miss Sears related that it was at this point she realized the eldress had never opened the door.

> Then I began to feel very strangely, and a wind seemed to pass over me, so that it blew my hair and I quickly went up the steps and rang the bell. Eldress Josephine opened the door. "Eldress, said I, "who was that eldress who went through this door a few minutes ago?" Eldress Josephine looked a little bit disturbed. "Nay, no one came through this door." "Oh yes they did," I answered, "and I called out to her several times, and she would not speak to me." "Oh nay," insisted Eldress Josephine, "No one has been here." "Eldress Josephine," I said very seriously, "someone has been here. It was an eldress, and she came right up to the door

and turned the handle and walked in. I was close to the screened door when she did it. I called to her, but she made no response."

Eldress Josephine kept muttering, "Oh nay, oh nay," but I saw Sister Annie Bell coming along the hallway, and I turned to her and said, "Sister Annie Bell, what eldress came through this door a few moments ago?" I saw her give a little glance to Eldress Josephine. "No eldress came through the door," she said. I saw too that she was a little disturbed. Then seeing that there was something being hidden from me I said, "Well now, if you two ladies will come into this room," pointing to the room on the left, "I would like to talk things over with you, for I can see that you both are disturbed. Now I wish to say that I saw with my own eyes an eldress standing at the foot of the steps and as I approached, I called to her, and she would not answer me, and she came and put her hand on the knob of the door and apparently walked in, but the moment she had done so, I said to myself, 'She did not open the door, she passed through it.' And now I think you should tell me the meaning of all this."

There was a long pause, and finally Eldress Josephine turned to Sister Annie Bell and whispered to her, and together they got up from their chairs and left the room. I could hear them whispering in the hall, and finally after a while they came into the room with a very solemn look upon their faces, Eldress Josephine, of course, leading. Then she spoke to me. "We have talked this thing over," she said. "Thee has read our journals, which no one of the world has seen before. We have trusted thee, and we know thee to be our friend, therefore I will speak with frankness. Thee did see someone coming through the door, and it was an Eldress, but she was not in the flesh, she was in the spirit. Many of us have seen her. She has walked around the house, and we have met her upon the stairs, but we did not think that anybody but a Shaker would be able to see her. It shows thee must be half a Shaker to have done so. We think she has come from the other world in protest to our having to sell the old Shaker Village, but we are all old, there is only a handful left, and we cannot afford to keep it."

85

Throughout the narrative, Miss Sears herself emerges with clarity. "Aren't you going to speak to me?" she asked peremptorily of the unfamiliar eldress. "I think you should tell me the meaning of all this," she demanded of Eldress Josephine. Knowing the Shakers very well, she more than suspected what their explanation would be and neither balked at hearing it nor let her friend continue to be evasive. In point of fact, this was an opportunity she had long hoped for. The manifestation left her bemused, but she knew enough of Shaker communion with the spirit world to have become a believer herself, and now she had the proof of her own eyes. Her progression toward this belief had been steady and gradual. Even before her association with the Shakers, she knew that feelings could be transmitted by extrasensory perception to friends with whom one was in particular sympathy. For her, such people were primarily those to whom she gave copies of *The Power Within*.

Before she had the little daybook printed, flowers fulfilled her need to know that thoughts were being sent to and from one or another of her acquaintances. One wrote to her, "The divine roses from your heart came to mine with such a thrill of understanding!" In the gardens of the Pergolas she planted larkspur and peonies to remind her of the pleasure she and Cousin Mary had in picking these blooms from the Endicott garden in Salem. "A dear old lady" from Boston and Nahant gave her some poppy seeds so that she could enjoy them year after year, "and when you see them nurture them in memory of me," the woman wrote, "for you may be sure then that your old friend is thinking of you." She meant from both this world and the next.

By 1916, the elders and eldresses of Harvard's Shaker Village knew that their dwindling community would have to be disbanded. In anticipation of that sad time they asked Miss Sears to undertake a book that would relate their history, and they also wished her to buy the oldest of their buildings in order to preserve it as a museum. Built in 1794, the structure had served the brethren as both office and living quarters. Just as the Fruit-lands farmhouse had been in need of restoration and happened to be situated within sight of the Pergolas' terrace, it again seemed a matter of chance that Miss Sears could move a local Shaker building and establish a second museum on Prospect Hill. In reality, though the timing was indeed a matter of chance, it was Miss Sears' readiness to seize opportunities and her sincere desire to listen and learn that prompted the Shakers to entrust her with the preservation of their history. It was a further credit to Miss Sears' understanding of them that when they left, Eldress Josephine, "with many tears," presented her the old hinge, hasp, and key leading to the Holy Hill where they would worship no more. Said Miss Sears of her relationship with the Shakers, "They had grown used to me and trusted me, and so they allowed me to go through all the old journals in their possession, telling of their visions upon what they called 'The Holy Hill of Zion,' where their sacred dances were held. In fact I was the first and only one to study the unabridged manuscripts written in pen and ink that told of the intimate details of what you might call their religious frenzy." The resulting book, *Gleanings from Old Shaker Journals*, was an important contribution to the chronicles of early America.

Miss Sears kept in touch with the eldresses after they moved to various other Shaker communities and was deeply moved when she was sent the gift of Eldress Josephine's bonnet upon her old friend's death. Clara Sears, in the 1940s, gave a gift of her own to the Canterbury, New Hampshire, Society of Shakers. Though she and most of the sisters had been born before the advent of electric lights, telephones, and automobiles, they welcomed those innovations, and the sisters therefore gratefully accepted a television set. Though it helped them pass the long winter days, a friend of Miss Sears was prompted to write, "It may be something of a shock to many of those sheltered Shakers to watch Hop-o-long Cassidy bang-a-te-banging along the trail and to listen to Kate Smith's moon come over the mountain. Possibly Eldress Emma may have to ban certain programs."

Radio was relatively primitive and television unheard of in 1916, when Houghton Mifflin published *Gleanings from Old Shaker Journals*. Working with the Harvard Shakers' old records, Miss Sears had become immersed in the events of the previous century. It was in 1843 that Alcott and his con-sociate family were at Fruitlands, and in reading the Shaker journals Miss Sears noted the frequency with which one or another of the Harvard transcendentalists visited the Shaker Village. They were particularly taken with the intellectual abilities of Elders Joseph Hammond and Joseph Myrick. In Miss Sears' words, as the elders were "endowed with great executive ability and powers of organization," it was no small wonder that Lane and Alcott "sought to converse with those who were so successfully solving the problem of a communistic life in direct contrast to their own endeavors." As the failure of Fruitlands became inevitable, Lane began to press Alcott to join the celibate Shaker society, and it was at this time that Louisa May Alcott wrote her impassioned diary entry, "I prayed God to keep us all together."

As Miss Sears expressed it in *Bronson Alcott's Fruitlands*,

> From now on clashing of wills disturbed the serenity of Fruitlands. Charles Lane, despondent over the course of events and the sense of failure, and seeing further financial complications in store for him, began seriously to consider the plan of life adopted by the Shakers whose well-filled corn-bins and full-rigged haylofts bespoke a system which provided plenty for man and beast, and gave time for alternate work and meditation. He began to talk of this to Mr. Alcott and urged him toward a more monastic life, and then suggested that they should join them. That he had great influence with Mr. Alcott is evident, and Mrs. Alcott, who fully realized this, grew restless and then alarmed.

Lane complained that Mrs. Alcott had "no spontaneous inclination towards a larger family than her own natural one...to keep all together she does and would go through a good deal of exterior and interior toil." Mrs. Alcott prevailed. As for Lane, he made good his intentions to join the Shakers, at least for a while, until his restless searchings bade him move onward. He did leave his son in their care for several years, however, having approached them on the matter on November 16, 1843, as recorded in their journal. "Lane the transcendentalist came here. Says he wants we should take his boy."

Until the practice became outmoded and even illegal in a new era of public responsibility, perpetuation of the celibate Shaker family was assured by the acceptance of orphans into their care. This unique concept of family, its composition and continuity, intrigued Miss Sears, who revered the childhood teachings of her grandmother and felt strong ties to her own traditional family but did not care for children. Two of her cousins, Clara and Fanny Payson, were brought up by the Peabody grandparents upon the early deaths of their parents. Fortunately for Miss Sears, who had no desire to play the role of the selfless maiden aunt, her own motherless niece and nephew were raised by their father (with household help of course) after the death of Mamie Sears Shaw. In later years Clara Sears and Miriam Shaw did become close companions, particularly after Mrs. Sears' death. Miriam established her own estate in Harvard and the two were chauffered about town by Sharples, a new behatted duo very much resembling the old.

Frank Shaw was overly protective of his daughter, who lamented the lack of an acceptable measure of freedom. Miss Sears sympathized and understood when Miriam, in her twenties and still living with her father, wrote as follows in thanking her aunt for a copy of *Gleanings from Old Shaker Journals*.

Dearest Auntie,

I'm deep in Mother Ann's adventures already.... Apart from any family bias, I think it really delightful and most vivid in atmosphere. This is just a hurried scrawl until I get a good opportunity to telephone. Being overheard is rather a bore and not condusive [sic] to conversation!

Clara Sears must have sensed early in life that child rearing was not to be her destiny. Neither she nor the cousins who were closest to her produced heirs. Like Clara, Fanny Mason never married. William Endicott and his wife were childless. Mary Endicott had no children by either Joseph Chamberlain or her second husband, William Hartley Carnegie, rector of St. Margaret's Church in London and chaplain to the House of Commons, whom she married two years after Mr. Chamberlain's death in 1914. Clara and Mary continued to correspond frequently. Mary, like Clara, was influenced by Clarissa Endicott Peabody's admonitions to make every day count and to give something from within. Since it was their shared philosophy that happiness came of activity, not passivity, Clara was glad when her cousin remarried and when "life was opened to [her] once more" as she immersed herself in Canon Carnegie's religious duties, "a new field for her."

With her move to Harvard, Clara Sears was exposed to experiences very different from those of Cousin Mary. She remained a devout Episcopalian but was able, in her ecumenism, to respond to untraditional influences. Miss Sears met the Shakers after the heyday of their shaking, speaking in tongues, and communing with the spirit world, when they had begun to lead lives more acceptable to outsiders, more understandable to the world. They tried to keep experiences of spiritual revelation to themselves and to share only their more rational symbolism. Fascinated by the symbolic aspect of Shaker religion, Miss Sears reflected this interest in her novel, *The Romance of Fiddler's Green*, in which a Shaker brother's cultivation of a symbolic garden brings about the redemption of the heroine's evil brother.

Appropriately, one of Miss Sears' favorite Shaker ceremonies concerned a farming image, the sowing of spiritual seed alongside that of the vegetables.

> The Brethren and boys would go forth with baskets full of the seeds they wished to plant, and all the morning they would sow row upon row, but would leave the earth piled up on one side, leaving the seed uncovered. They chose a day

without wind for doing this. Then when all the seeds were sown, the Sisters and the little foundling girls would go through the form of hanging imaginary baskets on their arms. The Eldresses would stand by and the Head Eldress would say, "Sisters, go forth now into the fields, and sow, where the Brethren have sown, the spiritual seeds of faith, love, truth, saintliness, that the material seed will take root in the ground, made sacred by the Spirit."

The old-time Shakers insisted that each child in their care learn a trade as well as the three R's. When the children reached their majority, they were allowed to stay or to leave the Shaker community, as they chose. Because of their sheltered existence, those who joined the world often had a hard time of it. Miss Sears felt that they were able to cope because of the "beautiful" Shaker conviction that work was a sacrament. Cooking, washing, and canning "filled them with a holy joy" and enabled even those who left the sect to deal with life's realities. The trades for which Shaker children were prepared followed traditional male and female expectations, but brothers and sisters were equal in respect, elders and eldresses equal in authority. Miss Sears' friends, Eldresses Josephine and Annie, were not subservient in any way but ran their own affairs in cooperative association with the elders.

Miss Sears regarded men and women as equals in intellectual spheres but held a conventional bias regarding more menial activities. She felt that a woman could associate herself with man's work but that the reverse was unacceptable. It was perfectly all right for Sister Tabitha Babbitt to invent the buzz saw by applying the insight gained from the circular motion of her spinning wheel; but when Miss Sears learned that one of her male employees was sewing in the evenings, she dismissed him summarily. On the other hand, she found no fault in assuming for herself the male prerogative of supervising construction of the Pergolas. Similarly, in the fall of 1920, she personally saw to the dismantling and reassembling of the old Shaker building she was having moved to its new site just above and across from the Fruitlands farmhouse. "Six weeks from the day we started," she boasted, "it was all up and painted and we started to move in the furniture," including the rocking chair that had been Mother Ann's while she was in Harvard in 1781. From the time of Miss Sears' move from Groton, it was never "they," but always "I" or "we" who saw projects through to completion.

Clara Sears liked to be in control in matters that were important to her. As for her intellectual life, she enjoyed the company of both male and female peers too greatly to be active in a cause unique to women. When women's suffrage was passed in 1920, she immediately registered as a Republican and exercised her franchise, but she had not involved herself in agitation for the bill. Nonetheless, in February of 1918 she warmed to the occasion of the fiftieth anniversary of the founding of the New England Women's Club, which had been established "amid scoffing and ridicule," she noted, with many women deterred from joining because of opposition by men in their families. "Men knew what Men's Clubs were," she said, "and not unnaturally supposed that Women's Clubs would be of the same nature, and much sarcastic advice as to quantity and quality of the liquors and tobacco to be provided was given in the papers." Miss Sears dismissed such philistines as insignificant, however, since the women had had strong support from such prominent thinkers as Ralph Waldo Emerson, Oliver Wendell Holmes, and John Greenleaf Whittier.

The First World War ended in November of 1918, and Miss Sears felt that the efforts of women had proved "a real factor" in the success of the allied cause. Her own patriotism had been galvanized by the hostilities. She served on the Boston committee of Lord and Lady Aberdeen's Bazaar, which raised thousands of dollars for a general fund for the allies and for aid to orphaned children in the British Isles. She was president of Harvard's Women's Guild, which sent six cases of hand-sewn and knitted goods to the war effort. Her most important contribution, however, utilized the practical Shaker skills she had been observing so attentively. She organized, in Harvard, a club for the canning and drying of food.

Responding to President Wilson's plea for preservation of food for both home and military purposes, Miss Sears enlisted the services of twelve local girls and engaged as manager Mrs. Frederick Avery, who had been brought up by Shakers but was now of the world and living in one of the houses no longer needed by the Harvard sect. Though pacifists, the Shakers who remained in the village gave their approval to the hundreds of cartons of canned and evaporated corn, pumpkins, beans, apples, pears, and peaches put up by their friend's Canning and Evaporating Club. They were particularly pleased with Miss Sears' interest in the preservation of food by evaporation, for they themselves were still baking excellent pies from apples dried eighteen years earlier. Since the club's workshop was located in a brick building near Mrs. Avery's home, the Shaker sisters who lingered in Harvard could visit frequently, "adding charm to the work," in the words of Miss Sears.

With patriotic fervor, Miss Sears expressed the club's ambitions to the *Boston Post.* "Think of the possibility of evaporating on a large scale. Give me one ship to load with vegetable foods and I will land the same amount for the boys over there that it takes 10 or 12 ships to carry at present." She rather overstated the statistics; one quart of evaporated fruit was the equivalent of four unprocessed quarts. Nonetheless, it was gratifying when Battery F, 303rd Heavy Artillery, Camp Devens, Ayer, purchased the year's output of the club, enough conserved fruits and vegetables to feed a company of 230 men for a month. With characteristic ceremony, Miss Sears arranged to have the food exhibited at the Town Hall before the Army took possession of it. The girls marched in singing a patriotic anthem Miss Sears had written, "The Unfurling of the Flag," and the goods were displayed "within a bower made of white birch poles trimmed with evergreen."

The twelve girls of the club also canned a thousand jars of food for their families' home consumption and taught their skills to others, just as Miss Sears herself went about the surrounding towns to encourage the organization of sister clubs so that the success of the Harvard group would not be an isolated example of what young women could do. A great deal of correspondence resulted from the whole project, so to guarantee the legibility of her letters, Miss Sears learned to typewrite, "staggering" Uncle George Peabody by the speed with which she taught herself and with the accuracy of her performance.

Miss Sears immersed herself in the war effort both physically and emotionally, and her patriotism was intensified by her ability to make a personal contribution. During the night of April 5, 1917, while Congress was debating a declaration of war, she awoke at about 2 a.m. "in a great state of agitation" although she was normally a sound sleeper. Lighting a candle, she went downstairs and walked aimlessly from room to room of the Beacon Street house, finally entering the library. "At this point," she related, "some vibration caught hold of my brain and used it for a means of expression." A phrase took possession of her, "It's the flag we've named Old Glory that's unfurling to the breeze," and she felt compelled to return to her room, where she dashed off the whole poem. When the morning paper came, she read about the actual declaration of war in a state of exhaustion resulting from what she considered a mystic experience. She wanted some good to come of her poem, so she had it printed, designating that proceeds from the sales should benefit the Red Cross. When its success soared beyond all expectations, it was set to music. To her immense gratification "The Unfurling of the Flag" for a time became a new national hymn, glorifying the war effort at rallies, stirring the children in schools, rousing religious fervor in churches. One clergyman's overblown paean no doubt appealed to Miss Sears' ecumenism.

It is a Baptist song because of its rugged love for freedom. It is a Unitarian song because of the clear intellectual statement of its patriotic faith. It is a Methodist song because of its warm, fervent patriotism of heart. It is a Catholic song because of its corporate embodiment of our nation in the Flag. It is a Congregational song because of its cultured reverence. It is an Episcopalian song because both words and music are almost like a liturgical prayer.

Members of the Authors' Club commended her efforts as enthusiastically as did the general public. Sara Ware Bassett, a novelist of the New England scene, wrote Miss Sears to say, "I know of no one who loves our country better.... Neither do I know of anyone who would do more for her." On the day of the Armistice, November 11, 1918, Clara Sears composed her personal prayer of thanks, "Peace Anthem," which was set to music as had been "The Unfurling of the Flag." A year and a half later, on Memorial Day of 1921, 15,000 thronged Fenway Park for a service in memory of the victims of the war, and Miss Sears' need for praise was amply gratified by the response of those in attendance. Among all the speeches, prayers, and hymns of the day, her anthem was one of those most applauded.

Between 1914 and 1921, with immense energy and versatility, Clara Sears had restored the Fruitlands farmhouse and compiled *Bronson Alcott's Fruitlands*; established a Shaker museum and written *Gleanings from Old Shaker Journals*; published her patriotic poems and pursued her war efforts; and still found time to write her first novel, *The Bell-Ringer*.

On June 18, 1921, Miss Sears welcomed members of the Authors' Club to its annual Pergolas luncheon and gave them a tour of the 127-year-old Shaker house, which held so many memories of the Harvard elders and eldresses. In thanking her hostess for a commemorative photograph of the assembled authors, Caroline Ticknor found words which were particularly apt when she marveled, "Every author is distinct as if he or she

95

has gone to have an individual picture taken. I think the spirit of the Shakers was pervading the atmosphere and helping to ensure the success of the reproduction."

If the Shakers were not also responsible for the success of Miss Sears' novels, they were unquestionably an influence upon the themes. In turning her attention to fiction, Miss Sears expanded her focus beyond the aristocracy into which she was born to write about the ordinary, often uneducated, New England country characters she had been observing closely for many years. Though her novels seem old-fashioned today, they were well received at the time and are worth reading for the quaint history Miss Sears was so anxious to preserve.

Chapter 7

Novels of the Nashaway

*When I started writing, I decided I would make
a greater impression if I wrote of one place....*
Clara Endicott Sears

As a novelist, Clara Sears was the local colorist of Harvard and its environs. The Nashua River placidly followed its course near the villages of Still River, Bolton, and Harvard. The plots of *The Bell-Ringer*, *The Romance of Fiddler's Green*, and *Whispering Pines* echoed local events of days gone by. History continued to dominate her interests and she desired, in her historical fiction, "to open wide the darkened portal leading to the Past and while we read, we walk beside the lives that once lived here, just as though it were the Present."

Miss Sears' characters spoke in dialect. She had a natural ear for inflection and had been jotting down snatches of conversation ever since recording Carolus Duran's reluctance to settle the business of payment for his 1895 portrait of her. Of more use to her later were conversations with the Shakers and the earthy remarks of Nashaway Valley characters such as Alonzo Willis of Groton. A small, spare man with thick gray hair, Willis used to wait at the nearby Ayer train station in his carryall in order to drive arriving passengers to their various destinations. Since he was known for his gift of quick retort, travelers looked forward to their rides with him and often led him on to tell all the local news. One day, after a bout of small talk, the Reverend Endicott Peabody's father remarked, "Well, Mr. Willis, you seem to know all the gossip going." Willis replied, "Lord sakes, why shouldn't I after driving all you Peabodys to and from the station all these years."

Alonzo Willis awakened Miss Sears' interest in the Harvard Shakers with a story about one of their number long before she had any notion of becoming friendly with them. Near the turn of the century, the sisters and brethren did not discourage the curious from being spectators at the dance which was part of their ritual. One day Willis and a companion joined the throng of onlookers, and the young friend found his attention drawn to a lovely Shaker sister. Sabbath after Sabbath he went to watch the Shakers in their religious dance, soon realizing that it was the young woman he was looking for. As Miss Sears recorded the tale,

Before he knew it he found himself very much in love though he had never spoken to the young woman and knew nothing about her. It began to prey upon him. He knew the consequences were very severe if any one of the Brethren or Sisters were found entertaining thoughts of love, so he took pains not to show his emotion, but he did not know womankind, nor their gift of divining what is going on in the masculine head, for the girl had noticed him and saw that he was on the lookout for her and this threw her into a tremendous state of emotion.

She thought it was sinful to even look at him, and yet finally she found herself unable to resist it. She went through torments day and night. If the slightest suspicion was awakened in the minds of the Elders, she knew she would be thrust out of the Society. The young man from Ayer had finally exchanged glances with her, and he also, realizing the situation, was in torment. So one day he confided all this to Alonzo Willis who was his great friend. It did not take Alonzo five minutes to solve the question. "Are you enough in love to want to marry the girl?" he asked. The young man from Ayer said that was what he longed for more than anything, but he was a rather sensitive being, prone to apprehensions. He began to enumerate all the stones that stood in that path of happiness. He had a New England conscience. She had her religion to think of, in which faith she was brought up. She might grow to despise him if she knew how ardently he loved her.

To all this Alonzo Willis said, "Pooh." He guessed he knew better. And one day he told his friend he had decided what they must do. In the first place they must find a buggy big enough to hold three if necessary. Then he and the young man from Ayer would drive to watch the Shaker Meeting, and when they came out of the Church for the Dance and the girl came dancing in their direction, he, Willis, would jump out of the buggy and seize hold of her and carry her to the buggy in his arms while his friend would have his horse keyed up to start the moment he and the girl reached it and got in, and then off they would go lickety split as fast as they could travel. They would take her to the home of the young man's sister, to whom he had already confided the plan, and she would have a dress ready for the girl to slip into, and they would roll up her Shaker dress and bonnet and leave them outside the door of the Church building some evening after dark, when the trick had been played. The sister also promised to get the clergyman of their church to be at the house when they arrived and marry them without further ado in case the Shakers pursued them and claimed her back into their fold. This all seemed wonderful to think of, but it filled the young man from Ayer with terror. All sorts of possibilities haunted him, and one day Alonzo Willis said to him that by rights he should be the one to carry her out from the dance, but he couldn't risk it, for six to one he'd be so full of doubts and fears that he would slump in the middle of it and the game would be up.

Well, the upshot of it was that the plan was decided on and one Sabbath afternoon they started out for the Shaker Village. They got there a few moments before the Shakers came out for the dance and Willis' whole time was taken up bolstering his friend up for the coming climax. As he was doing this the Church doors opened and one by one the

99

Shakers filed out, the Sisters by one door and the Brethren by the other, and they took their positions on the lawn. Both young men saw that the Shaker Maiden was aware of their presence and that her face was very pale. The Brethren began to sing and swerve around in a circle. The Sisters did likewise, and when the young Shaker girl swerved around their way, Alonzo Willis leapt from the buggy and seizing the girl around the waist he hoisted her up in the air and dashed back with her to his friend, and jumping in with the girl between them they started off at a breakneck pace for Ayer. A howl went up from the Shakers. The Brethren shouted! The Sisters screamed! The buggy dashed on, its occupants feeling that the whole horde of Shakers were after them in hot pursuit.

When they reached the sister's house Alonzo Willis jumped out, prepared to fight any Elder or Eldress for that matter who might lay hold on the girl, when to his surprise he found the road over which they had come empty. There was no sign of a Shaker anywhere! But thinking they might be hiding in ambush, they hurried the girl into the house. She was almost fainting with terror but as eager as they to get the knot tied. The clergyman was an accommodating soul and did not even wait for the girl to put on the dress prepared for her by the young man's sister, but had them stand up before him as they were, dusty and disheveled from their precipitous drive, and in a very few minutes he pronounced them to be man and wife. Everyone heaved a sigh of relief. "If they come now," Willis said, "they won't get nowhere. The knot's tied, and they can't untie it no matter what." But they did not come.

This strange courtship appears unlikely, but the truth of the story was verified by Eldress Josephine when Miss Sears came to know her well enough to inquire. The couple lived a happy life, to the evident delight of Willis, who often interrupted his telling of the tale to exclaim, "My land! If those Shakers didn't raise a yell when they saw me running off with the girl. You could have heard 'em from here to Calcutta."

Clara Sears used such local tales and country accents for the plots and dialogue of her three novels. From the distance of years and the safety of spinsterhood, she depicted highly idealized love relationships. Myrtle Stone, the chaste heroine of *The Romance of Fiddler's Green*, like Clara Sears, was of a serious nature and did not care to "toy with love." Upon finding it, Myrtle "almost dreaded its bondage." In *The Bell-Ringer*, love finds its perfection in an unconsummated union. In the words of the heroine, "It's the understanding and sympathy that counts and that lasts."

Miss Sears drew this plot from a story related to her by an elderly Still River woman who had been the childhood neighbor of Louisa May Alcott during the months immediately following the Alcotts' retreat from Fruitlands. The novel tells of a spiritual bond between Seth, the village bell ringer, and Faith, a pure, crippled maiden. The hero tolls his church bells, some say with help from the spirit world, in celebration of platonic love. Utopia is attainable because the couple keeps their love on an other-worldly plane instead of subjecting it to the vicissitudes of every-day life. Miss Sears wrote in her preface,

> Wherever you look among the old traditions of the Nashua Valley there is nearly always uppermost the search for spiritual attainment and the reaching-out for some desired ideal. And so it was with Seth, the village bell-ringer, - a transcendentalist, though he did not know the word.

A *New York Tribune* reviewer noted, "New England legends and the New England temperament, as still found in some remote, secluded vales, lend themselves wondrously to the semi-supernatural and to psychological extravaganza." He found the novel "a Puritan romance of indescribable sweetness, tenderness and pathos; not devoid of humor; touched here and there with the grimness of the old Puritan character; with some powerfully dramatic passages and invested throughout with haunting mystery."

The Bell-Ringer was published in 1918 and reflected the mysticism which had been nurtured under the influence of her eldress friends.   Clara Sears was attuned to the otherworldly overtones of Seth's story as it was told to her, and she was prepared to welcome any such experiences that might come her own way. During one of the daily drives she and her mother enjoyed together, an old Still River house captured her attention, and she wrote of the resulting experience on the pages of a private letter. Her matter of fact description belied its mystical nature and typified Miss Sears' pragmatic approach to the unknown.   She was, as always, insistent upon having her own way and thereby got to the heart of the matter.

There was something of a fascination about it to me, so much so that I used to stop the motor and gaze and gaze at it and wish that I could go in there to see what the house was like. One day when I was taking my mother to drive and we passed by the old Howard place, I stopped the car and jumping out went over to the front door and knocked. After a while a man from the next house came over and said there was no one living in that house, and had not been living there for a long while. I asked him to let me in to see the inside of it, as I felt sure the walls were stencilled, and I was very anxious to see the woodwork.   But he refused point blank to let me in.

One day some time after that when I was passing there and looking at the old house, I suddenly saw the curtain lifted and the face of a young woman looking out. I stopped the motor at once and said to my mother, "Now is my chance. There is someone in the old Howard house." So I quickly got out and went to the door and knocked vigorously. No one answered, but I saw the curtain shake and became persuaded that the young woman was still behind it, so I knocked again. No answer. Then I knocked again. Still no answer. But I still was not to be frustrated, so I went on knocking and finally knocked at the window. The man from the adjoining house came over and said to me, "There's no one living in that house." "Oh yes there is," I said, "for I saw a young woman lift the curtain and look out of the window."

102

But still he answered, "There's no one living in that house, and there hasn't been for many years past. I know, for I have the keys, and no one else has them." But still I persisted. I said I wanted to see the stencilled walls inside, and he replied, "I've never seen any stencilled walls. I don't believe there are any." I said, "Yes, there are."

After much wrangling, I gained my point. I said, "There is somebody inside that house." And he said, exasperated, "Well, seeing as you feel that way, I'll let you in." So I went in confident that in the room on the right-hand side of the door I would find the young woman who had looked through the curtain. I entered the door ready to give a morning's greeting, but I found the room empty. I said to the man, "She must have gone into another room," and he replied, "I told you there was no one in this house, and there never has been for years and years." I then insisted upon going all over the house. I even looked into every closet, but they were empty. I glanced up at the walls in the hall and I found them beautifully stencilled. It must have been second sight, for I had never been inside the house and had never heard what it was like. I left it with extreme regret and disappointment. But there was one thing sure - I had seen a young woman looking through that window behind the curtain in the room on the right-hand side of the front door.

That afternoon she recounted her strange experience to an old Still River resident, probably the same woman who had enthralled her with the tale of the bell ringer. Long years ago, she was told, a young bride from Boston who had come to the house was frightened by its isolation and by the deep woods surrounding it. There were no near neighbors, only wildcats, bears, and foxes, which further terrified her. The occasional passer-by saw her face at the window, lifting the curtain, peering out of the window of the room on the right-hand side of the front door. "So," proposed Miss Sears' informant, "it must be that the young woman you saw peering out was the ghost of that little wife who died a very few years after her marriage."

Such tales did not overpower Miss Sears' practical temperament, but she believed that certain people, at certain times, were privileged to catch vibrations of former days. This belief was not new to her. She had held herself open to such phenomena as long ago as her solitary visit to Joan of Arc's cell in Rouen; she had sentimentally imagined some kind of thought waves from the Fruitlands transcendentalists. Her experience of the Shaker eldress who was not of the flesh but of the spirit had convinced her of "powers lying fallow in the mind and in the unexplored regions of the soul;" the ghost of the little wife merely confirmed what she already knew.

Miss Sears used neither of her mystical experiences as plot for a novel, but she shared with the Shakers a belief in salvation through work and faith and she drew on the flower symbolism with which they expressed this outlook. As she phrased it in *Gleanings from Old Shaker Journals*, Shakers "looked upon life as a garden filled with flowers and weeds, and they were required to weed the garden of their souls as conscientiously as they would weed a flower garden, and keep the ground stirred and nourished by good thoughts and kind deeds, and gentle speech." In *The Romance of Fiddler's Green*, published in 1922, Brother Simeon plants a garden in the center of which is a circle of golden marigolds, "for yellow is the color o' the sun and gives thee health, and the circle means Eternity." The kindly Shaker lures the evil Zeke to labor in this symbolic garden so that hard work and understanding may accomplish his redemption from sin. The plan succeeds, although not without difficulty. Brother Simeon's efforts are complicated by the tendency of the superstitious townspeople to attribute eerie happenings to Shaker spirits rather than to Zeke's cruel pranks.

Because of her rustic New England settings, her concern for spiritual essence, and her use of symbolism, Clara Sears' work was inevitably compared with Hawthorne's. The *Boston Herald* commented, "not that Miss Sears is in any way imitating or copying Hawthorne, but that the reader feels that Hawthorne would have loved to utilize the unusual material which Miss Sears handles with marked distinction."

Miss Sears sent copies of all her novels to a friend of Nahant days, Henry Cabot Lodge. She felt such pride in his response to *The Romance of Fiddler's Green* that she had his letter framed and hung in the library at the Pergolas. In part, it read,

> I am again struck by your penetrating knowledge and sympathetic comprehension of our native New Englander. Their shrewdness, humor, strong sense, sometimes hard, are known to all who have looked upon them with considerate eyes. Their great qualities which are many, and the exceptions with a capability for cold viciousness are also known to those who have studied them and their history. But I can think of no one who in literature, with the exception of Hawthorne, has felt and understood and depicted the strain of mysticism in the New Englander of the true old stock so admirably as you.

Nonetheless, her fiction has not endured as have her works on Fruitlands and the Shakers or her later works on Indians and nineteenth century American art. In truth, her characterizations lack Hawthorne's depth and intensity, qualities essential if the obscure lives of simple country folk are to be immortalized. Her descriptive passages, however, are often written, in the words of a *Boston Transcript* reporter, "quite in the Hawthorne cadenced prose." He included in his review the opening passages of *The Bell-Ringer.*

> It is at the close of a Sabbath day, at sundown, when the air is still, that one should listen for the bells. Their voices can be heard ringing across the intervale from one hill-town to another - calling and answering all along the whole valley of the Nashua. As a rule Lancaster starts first, and a deep tone from the belfry of the old Bulfinch steeple reverberates in the hush of the magic hour.

There comes a momentary pause - then the faint, far-away sound of the bells of Fitchburg, and the bells of Leominster, of Lunenburg and Shirley can be heard ringing a chain of silver notes into the mellow afterglow, and out from the steeples of Still River, Harvard, and the towns along the eastern ridges pour the answers like a wave of crystal music - and back and forth, back and forth, peal the bells across the intervale at sundown.

Generations come and go and listen for their sweet-toned voices - but it is not every one who can hear them, and few there are that note the difference in their chiming, or stop to ponder upon their mystic language; for they are human hands that toll the bells, and through these hands flows blood from human hearts, and who can tell the mysteries hidden therein?

Whispering Pines, Miss Sears' third and last novel, was published in 1930, the year following her mother's death. It is in this novel that the young maiden is troubled about accepting the marriage proposal of her beloved because of the bonds of duty given, albeit lovingly, to her ailing mother. Miss Sears herself had made no substantial sacrifices in choosing to live with her mother, with whom she had a good relationship marked by respect and affection. In fact, living with her mother was rather more helpful to her needs than otherwise.

Whispering Pines was set in Harvard just prior to World War I, and in it Miss Sears continued to write of New England days gone by. She sought to preserve the picture of a girl who was narrow in her views of life and had few interests outside the home, a young woman who no longer existed because the war and war work had broadened her outlook. As Miss Sears observed in a press interview, "The lid was off, and no matter what happened afterwards, the point of view was changed. Before the war, they did not have many automobiles and, of course, no radios. They lived shut off by themselves in their villages, but now nothing happens that they don't know about. The country girl makes up like her city sister; she listens to the same radio and her interests are no longer confined to her little village."

Clara Sears felt that she knew such girls well, having worked so closely with them in the Canning and Evaporating Club during the war years. Club sessions had been fertile ground for gossip. Miss Sears listened attentively to the girls' romantic revelations and noted their accents as deliberately as she had stored away the voice and idiosyncrasies of Alonzo Willis. By her own admission, she hired local people for her various building projects as much for convenience as to furnish herself with "a supply of characteristics that can not be improved upon." It amused her when one of the men working on the construction of her cloister asked another, "What's she going to do here, anyway?" And the other replied, "I dunno; keep her apples here, I guess."

Interaction with others was a large part of Miss Sears' daily life, though action might be the more appropriate term. She ordered; others hastened to obey. She had a substantial household staff, which was supplemented by caterers for her larger luncheons. She kept in daily touch with her farmer and the men who cared for the grounds and gardens of the Pergolas. She hired and supervised the docents for her museums and saw to the maintenance of the buildings that housed the exhibits. All this was in addition to the creative work of restoration, research, and writing. While in residence at the Pergolas, Miss Sears had so little time to herself during the day that she usually took an hour's rest after the evening meal and then wrote until two in the morning. The novelist Alice Brown wrote from Beacon Hill to caution her against this practice. "Please don't write at night! I don't dare. Indeed, I am as polite to my sleepy body as if it were a heathen god."

During Boston winters at 132 Beacon Street, where her mother continued to hold the household keys, Miss Sears was able to write in the morning. In the hushed atmosphere of the nearby Boston Athenaeum, she joined Emilie Loring and Sara

Ware Bassett almost daily for several quiet hours. On the fifth floor of this intellectual sanctuary, each of the authors had a private alcove in which to write. Fresh flowers and peaceful surroundings were so predictably assured that the *Boston Herald* made much of the time the inviolate rule of silence was interrupted.

A family of squirrels scampered in from the balcony and went on a rampage which sent them up and down the room, over tables and chairs, then out to the grilled balcony again. Though, to some, this might seem an incident of relative unimportance, to those who were present the day it occurred it was a memorable one. So shocking was the interruption, so unheard of the cause of it, that things have been more or less dated by it ever since. "I think I finished my last chapter before the squirrels came in day.... Wasn't it a few days after the squirrels came that he addressed the Authors' Club? "

With her new colleagues, Clara Sears could combine social and professional interests into a congenial whole. There were meetings featuring informative talks by writers, critics, and publishers; there were occasional luncheons and dinners; there were exchanges of useful comments on works in progress. Her author friends must have been aware of the insecurity which surfaced each time Clara Sears submitted a new manuscript. Despite the successes of *Bronson Alcott's Fruitlands, Gleanings from Old Shaker Journals, The Bell-Ringer,* and *The Romance of Fiddler's Green,* Clara Sears did not have the confidence in her writing that she had in her museums. In September of 1923, she meekly delivered to Houghton Mifflin her manuscript on William Miller, *Days of Delusion.* She wrote self-effacingly in her Line-A-Day diary that they "were very nice to me," hardly the assured attitude of a published author. Ten days later, a flattering acceptance restored her confidence, and when the book came out in the spring Judge Grant sent a note that confirmed the good opinions of others.

Dear Miss Clara,

The book is excellently done and adds another valuable chapter to your record of New England's pathetic spiritual eccentricities.

Miss Sears received her first professional setback in 1926, a year before her mother's operation for cancer. In August of that year she brought Houghton Mifflin her new novel, *Nephew Dave*. Although her editor, Ferris Greenslet, "was very cordial and kind in receiving it," he did not accept the manuscript for publication. With a new title, *Whispering Pines*, she had it privately printed four years later. Emilie Loring declared herself so taken with its descriptive passages that she had to put it aside for a few days lest the "Harvard atmosphere" creep into her own novel. Although Miss Sears depicted the turbulence as well as the peace of Harvard's hills and fields with feeling and competence, her characters were stereotypical and her plot melodramatic - perfect material for the grade B "Eastern" it nearly became.

The "talking screen" was of more than casual interest to Miss Sears and her friend Sara Ware Bassett. Hollywood produced one of Miss Bassett's novels, *The Taming of Zenas Henry*, under the title *Captain Hurricane*. In 1931, Miss Sears gave an agent permission for the filming of *Whispering Pines* and for any adaptations that might be necessary, but negotiations did not proceed beyond the preliminaries.

Clara Sears did not attempt another novel, and wisely so, for her talent lay with the facts of history, not with their incorporation into fiction. She returned, instead, with unqualified success, to the documentation of local history. This time the impetus was her chance discovery of Indian arrowheads by the Nashua River, at the bottom of her hill; and again her well-known initiative set her to researching a new book and founding the third museum of the Fruitlands and Wayside Museums, Incorporated.

Chapter 8

Star-Shooter

We advised you to make composition [compensation]
of the salvages [savages] as did pretend any title
or lay claim to any of the land within the territories
granted to us by his majesty's charter....

Massachusetts Bay Company Second Letter
of Instruction to Governor Endicott

Endicotts and Peabodys continued to interweave the fabric of their past and present lives at Glen Magna, The Farm. On June 22, 1930, to celebrate the tercentenary of the landing of John Winthrop at Salem, Clara's cousin William Endicott, who now owned The Farm, held a family party there, an occasion duly noted by Clara in her Line-A-Day. In honor of his paternal ancestor, John Endicott, who had greeted Governor Winthrop three hundred years earlier when he arrived on the *Arbella* with the royal charter and seals, William Endicott had a medal struck. One side depicted the head of Governor Endicott, the other his famous pear tree.

For Clara Endicott Sears, now almost seventy, the hospitality of The Farm and the affection of cousins William and Mary represented the continuity of her life. Family bonds had recently taken on added importance as Clara was still adjusting to the death of her mother the previous August, at the age of ninety-three. Mrs. Sears had been ill with cancer for a number of years, necessitating round-the-clock nurses, and her daughter made frequent references to the state of Mamma's health in her Line-A-Day. On the first page of this five-year diary she penned the phrase *lares et penates* to indicate that the little book would be an unrevealing record of daily events and not a disclosure of deeply felt emotions.

Few people realized that Miss Sears was concerned about her own health during the 1920s, but she frequently interspersed her domestic jottings with notations about a growth on her back. She went regularly to a favorite Peabody family physician, Sidney Ellis, and on his advice in October of 1923, she began daily applications of iodine. Four years later she was still using the iodine to keep *it* in check, and her weight had decreased from 117 to 110 pounds. "Am much thinner than I was at first so it shows more but I do not think it is any bigger in reality." There are no diaries documenting the last twenty years of her life and therefore no further information about this medical problem, but she did continue to see Dr. Ellis frequently for unrelated osteopathic treatments. Along with the iodine, she continued her daily spiritual medicine as prescribed by *The Power Within*, putting concerns about herself in the background.

Her mother's health was a constant worry, and Sara Ware Bassett also became seriously ill. Miss Sears sent her flowers and wrote cheerful notes with amusing anecdotes of the cows getting into the vegetables. Miss Bassett appreciated her friend's attentiveness to the needs of others and replied, "Sometimes I think you were born...to cheer people and give them strength to go on." Both knew that Miss Sears' burdens weighed heavily upon her. Her mother could not live much longer, and indeed for many years following Mrs. Sears' death Clara's seriousness of purpose overpowered all sense of humor.

On Mrs. Sears' eighty-ninth birthday, in July of 1925, those around her were "careful not to refer to it," and by the summer of 1927 a rapid progression of the cancer obliged her daughter to resign as vice president of the Boston Authors' Club "owing to sickness at my house." At the end of September the two women cut short their stay in Harvard and made an urgent move to Boston. As is often the case, the patient bore up with an equanimity impossible for Clara, who prayed she might never again have such a distressing twenty-four hours as those that preceded the operation. Restless and distraught, unable to wait idly by, she asked Sharples, the chauffeur, to drive her back to the Pergolas with the excuse that they needed fresh vegetables, apples, and pears. Mary Carnegie left Bar Harbor hastily in order to be of what help she could, and Fanny Mason came from her summer home in Walpole, New Hampshire, to comfort Clara. Mrs. Sears' spirits remained "unquenchable," and Clara marveled at her mother's tenacious hold on life. A remarkable recovery allowed her another two years of life, albeit under continued nursing care at home.

Less than a year after Mrs. Sears' surgery, Mary Carnegie was stricken with influenza and pneumonia, thus adding to Clara's anxieties. Cables flew back and forth between London and Boston until the crisis had passed. The protracted stress undermined Clara's own health. Sara Ware Basset advised her not to give of herself at the expense of her own well-being, since she was the "corner-stone" of her family. Miss Bassett feared for her friend, although she knew that Miss Sears was usually able to renew herself from the natural beauty surrounding the Pergolas and from her power within. Miss Bassett also knew that Clara's habitual route to recovery was through work, and she was soon to see welcome evidence of this healing process.

Local history was once again the impetus for new projects. In the spring of 1928, Indian arrowheads came to the surface during some plowing that was being done in Miss Sears' orchard. The discovery "fired my curiosity," she wrote, "and I began looking into the history of the Nashaway Valley and the Indian lore." She was filled with a desire to gather all possible relics, and word spread, as word will do in small towns. Farmers were not surprised when a liveried Sharples drove the Pierce Arrow into their barnyards unannounced and opened the door for an eager, white-haired patrician who inevitably asked whether they had found any "strange looking stones."

She must have felt some Great Spirit was looking after her when, coincidentally, a group of archaeologists camped near her property while searching for Indian artifacts along the Nashua River. Miss Sears delved right in and dug with them, sixty-six year old blue blood that she was, and was jubilant when she found a tomahawk at the foot of her very own property. The great depression was imminent and a local reporter later imagined her "in her Hooveralls, or whatever other outdoor costume she wears for digging...although even a stranger would recognize as an aristocrat the lady who spoke with such unaffected charm." Charm or not, the household gods, *lares et penates*, had apparently not fallen under its influence, for in September of 1928 she injected an uncharacteristically pessimistic note into her Line-A-Day. "Wrote to Mr. West in answer to his letter that if we were all alive in the spring I should want him to paint the house as usual at the usual price."

The household moved back to 132 Beacon Street in mid-October, and Miss Sears' spirits revived through the winter as she initiated a nationwide search for Indian relics. Six volumes of related correspondence ultimately accumulated. She wanted her new museum to be educational; to include artifacts from tribes of all regions in North America; and, though small, "to be able to hold its own with the best, as regards authenticity." In this undertaking, she was entering a field completely new to her, one in which help was less readily available than it had been for her transcendentalist and Shaker projects; but she was an amateur, a lover, in the highest sense and, to her credit, sought professional advice and knowledgeable authentication for the Indian

113

objects she acquired. True to form, she had neither curator nor secretary, continuing to do everything herself until 1930, the year following her mother's death, when she incorporated her museums and selected trustees to ensure continuity in the event of her own death. At that time she also began to form close bonds with two younger women, her niece Miriam, who had bought an estate in Harvard, and Dr. Ellis' daughter, Virginia, who became her part-time secretary and helped with the research and typing of *The Great Powwow*.

In the meantime, if her correspondence sometimes betrayed an unprofessional eagerness, the occasional dealer who suspected an easy mark soon received his comeuppance. One such was a Mr. Newman of Cedar Rapids, Iowa, from whom she bought a great many items, most of which were authentic, but not all. When he sent some gem-points that were not genuine she wrote, "Now I want you to realize that all that goes into my collection has to receive the endorsement of the Peabody Museum at Harvard College. Those gem or jewel-points have been rejected as doubtful specimens. This was a great blow to me." Since she had bought them at her own risk, she did not ask him to take them back; but, after a year of sending her acceptable feathered bonnets, beaded vests, stone implements, and weapons, he again fell from grace. A belt he said was an old one was "no such thing." She fired off a letter to say, "You are dreaming. I can go down any day to the London Harness Co. on Tremont St., and buy a leather belt with a shiny buckle just like the one you have sent, and cover it with a bead strip and it would be no different." This time she wanted her check back "without delay."

In her search for Sioux items, Miss Sears was greatly helped by Dr. Ellis, who also summered in Harvard and who was keenly interested in Indian lore. While on his annual fall hunting trip to North Dakota, he sought out Col. A. B. Welch, who was in charge of Indian affairs and was, incidentally, the foster son of a Sioux chief. This was an auspicious contact as Col. Welch was able not only to "get some wonderfully interesting things" for Miss Sears but also to guide this somewhat naive Boston lady.

The two became acquainted by mail, and in her first letter Miss Sears emphasized that she considered it "of the utmost importance to secure and spread a knowledge of the past, and of the race to which this country belonged." She gave him her *bona fides* as she did with all her suppliers. "I realize that being a total stranger to you, you may have misgivings in regard to my request. If you have such a thing as a copy of 'Who's Who' where you are, you will find out all about me, but if not, you can write to The New England Trust Company, 135 Devonshire St., Boston, Mass., and they will assure you that you will be quite safe in dealing with me in a business way."

As they continued to correspond, Col. Welch found in her a kindred spirit who appreciated the symbolic. "Like yourself," he wrote, "I like those things...with mystic qualities." The sun, he told her, symbolized the Great Spirit, and the rock his abiding strength. Health was intimately connected with religion, and a healthy body was proof of the favor of the Great Spirit. Since such a philosophy was akin to her own, Miss Sears decided to incorporate the symbols of the rock and the sun into her projected Indian Museum. In the middle of the building she planned to place the finest boulder she could find from her pasture and then have rays or vibrations carved into the concrete floor and painted yellow.

When Miss Sears purchased artifacts from Col. Welch, whose Indian name was Charging Bear, she had no need to consult her expert advisors regarding their authenticity. He bought them directly from Indian friends and explained to her that prices were difficult to estimate in advance since such purchases took "the aspect of quite a diplomatic exchange of compliments and sweetly flowing diplomatic terms of regrets and inquiry regarding age, bravery, coups of valor."

Fortunately, Col. Welch insisted on authenticity in every aspect of her museum. Miss Sears had commissioned from New York's Museum of Natural History several figures on which she planned to put Indian garments. She was well aware that tribes differed in their bone structures, facial characteristics, and of course dress; but, lacking proper garb for a Nashaway Indian, she apparently was willing to make do. Col. Welch wrote her sternly, "Don't place Sioux leggins on him and expect to have an Indian student believe that they are Algonkin."

In February of 1929, Col. Welch sent Miss Sears a manuscript he had written "more for preservation of historical events than for publication." In it he described an expedition led by Col. Leavenworth, in which his foster father, Chief Gras, had participated. Col. Welch was clearly "out of sympathy with the white men of those early days" and wanted to reinstate the integrity of the Indian views, much as she was preparing to do in *The Great Powwow*. She passed the winter of 1929 doing research for the book, securing Indian artifacts, and supervising the moving of an old clapboard schoolhouse and its conversion into a museum for the display of her treasures. The opening in June was subdued, for Mrs. Sears' days had become "pretty mean," and radium treatment had been prescribed. Although she showed the museum off to the Authors' Club early that summer, following their annual luncheon on the terrace of the Pergolas, "Mother did not feel up to coming downstairs to meet them, but she watched them wandering about the place from her window."

Once the radium treatment had begun, Miss Sears sensed her mother's end and began to lose her composure. She and one of the nurses "had a crash," and the woman left her employ although she had been with them for several years. Furthermore, Mr. Newman of Cedar Rapids chose this inopportune time to intrude, sending an opal with the request that she have it set for him in a gold eagle's claw. She was appalled and begged "to state that there are no such jewelers here, and that I am amazed at your even suggesting such a thing." Unbelievably, he proceeded

116

to ask her for a loan of money. This was not the first time he had done so, but it was the last, as she finally convinced him that she found such behavior beyond bad taste. "It is useless for you to waste stamps making any such request for I shall never loan you a cent of money. Please to remember this, and not trouble me in such an ungentlemanly manner."

Col. Welch, on the other hand, was a gentleman who wrote to her as a friend. He shared her "joy of success" in the excellent notices from Boston papers and museum curators regarding the Indian Museum; and as he learned more about her, he understood how gratifying it was for her "to realize the completion of your dreams to preserve those mysticisms of yesterday." He hesitated to write a letter of condolence at the time of Mrs. Sears' death in the late summer of 1929, waiting instead until the following January because he felt the need to study "the propriety of acquainting you with a few thoughts which might be of comfort, but after all, I am of the west and its crudeness and direct approach, and you with your paternal and maternal ancestors' influences quite scared me and gave me a wrong complex. I know you better now."

When Mrs. Sears began "slipping down hill fast," Miriam Shaw and William Endicott joined Clara, off and on, at the Pergolas. On August 26 Clara noted in her Line-A-Day that Mrs. Sears had "a sort of shock towards evening and was unable to speak. She could make a noise but we could not understand her. It was terrible.... Morphine had no effect. I did not know anything could be so terrible." Dr. Ellis and Clara were with her when she died at 9:45 the following morning.

Since Knyvet Sears' death thirty-eight years before, the two women had lived their lives closely together with respect and affection, and Clara felt the loss of her mother keenly. Work, as usual, was her refuge and her salvation. Although she returned to Harvard for the remainder of summer and the autumn, Sharples drove her back to Boston frequently so that she could see to the much-needed redecoration of 132 Beacon Street.

Refurbishing the house was a practical means of acknowledging her loss and dealing directly with her grief while keeping herself as busy as possible. Her Line-A-Day indicates that she was exhausted. One day, while at the town house "intending to do a lot of work," she was so tired she lay down on her sofa "and slept until the motor came!" When she and the household staff moved to town at the end of October, the sense of finality, upon entering the house without her mother, was overwhelming. When she saw that the two servants already in residence had "tears running down their cheeks," she came to the full realization that she was now truly alone.

It was her choice to remain so from then on. Emilie Loring was once saddened to see Clara standing by herself in her doorway, waving good-bye, but was comforted "when I think that if you didn't want to be alone, you wouldn't be, and I feel a little better." After her mother's death a friend wrote, "Her memory will remain as a benediction and a blessing on the beauty everywhere set forth so eloquently about the Pergolas." Clara believed this to be true and did not try to people the Pergolas with guests in order to fill what others perceived as a void in her life. Quite the reverse. Loneliness and solitude are not identical. She had her human share of loneliness and counted on her luncheons to help keep it at bay; she valued solitude to such an extent that only Mary Carnegie and, later, Miriam Shaw were ever invited to be overnight guests at the Pergolas.

After her mother's death, Clara became better acquainted with her cousin, Philip Sears, who had left a business career late in life to nurture his talent as a sculptor. He became particularly well known for his figures of athletes, and at about the time of Mary Sears' death, he conceived the notion of sculpting a young Indian brave. Philip Sears' life was not without tragedy, for his son died while still a young man. In her Line-A-Day for December 22, 1923, Miss Sears had written, "News came today of David Sear's death in Paris," and she knew that Philip felt his son's spirit had inspired him in the sculpting of *Pumunangwet, He-Who-Shoots-the-Stars.* Cousin Clara had not commissioned the piece, but when she saw it she made an immediate offer of purchase. Philip was delighted, especially because the bigger-than-life casting would be placed in front of the Indian Museum and have a dramatic backdrop in nearby Mt. Wachusett as well as the New Hampshire mountains to the north.

Pumunangwet was cast in specially tinted bronze and, thanks to an inspiration of Miss Sears, was placed not on a pedestal but on a much more suitable base of Nashaway Valley rock. It was "a splendidly-poised figure of an Indian, standing firmly and looking into the sky after the arrow, which he has shot from the bow." To Miss Sears it symbolized aspiration and, as she happily discovered, actually did depict a custom common to local Indians at the time of the vernal equinox. On the spring day of equal darkness and light, an Algonquin brave "would be sent onto a bit of high ground to shoot upward at the stars" in anticipation of hopes and goals for the year to come. In the invocation which Miss Sears composed for the dedication she wrote, "You have shot so high that it has reached immortality...." It is not unlikely that she took private pleasure in knowing that her growing museum complex would ensure her own small piece of immortality, that she was a star-shooter in her own right.

The unveiling of *Pumunangwet* took place on June 12, 1931. Chief Buffalo Bear of the Sioux was the guest of honor, "a very commanding figure in an elk skin suit and three eagle's feathers in his hair." After the meal, in preparation for the ceremony, he "swathed" his body in a dark blue cloak ornamented with bands of Sioux embroidery and donned a headdress of 136 eagle's feathers, which reached the ground. The procession was a mixture of patriotism and symbolism; bugles and drums sounded as Boy and Girl Scouts escorted Chief Buffalo Bear to the statue and stood by while Philip Sears and the chief smoked a pipe of peace, blowing the smoke into the air in eternal friendship. When the bugler sounded reveille "to awaken the soul of the statue," David

Buffalo Bear lifted his arms and shouted "Awake! Awake, - Algonquin brother!" and the blankets fell from the statue just as the sun pierced through "great battle clouds" and "threw a shaft of light right down upon the shooting Indian." The crowd "stood as if transfixed." The statue looked alive at that moment, the very color of the bronze emphasizing the illusion. "The people looked at it in a sort of hushed surprise."

Two more festive dedications took place during the 1930s. In 1932, a new wing was added to the Indian Museum, and the whole complex was properly dedicated at last. Again Miss Sears preserved an old colonial building, this time a barn, moving it to abut the schoolhouse, which she had faced with bricks from the original town hall of nearby Lancaster. She faced the new structure with bricks from a Harvard College building that was being altered.

Miss Sears invited Wo Peen, a young Pueblo Indian artist, to dance at the grand opening which, as usual, was laden with symbolism. Wo Peen and Chief Buffalo Bear chanted her invocation, "Summoning the Lights," from each of the four compass points. They spoke in an Indian tongue, with the English language verses printed for the guests in their programs, and prayed that the sun might warm the building with gold, that the moon might tip its corners with silver. "May it be Holy Mellow Ground."

Kate Cotharin of the Massachusetts Indian Association congratulated Miss Sears on "a glorious contribution toward a saner view of the Indian" and relayed some high praise from David Buffalo Bear and Wo Peen. "The Indians didn't see how you could have made the symbolic so Indian." As they stood to be photographed after the ceremony, Miss Sears and the two men "looked like royalty," all three ramrod straight, the Indians in feathered headdress, Miss Sears tiny by comparison as she stood between them but holding her own in a print dress and fashionable cloche hat. Over the years, Miriam Shaw began to observe that her aunt was assuming excessive airs of royalty as she held almost daily court in front of one or another of her museums. The homage paid her by total strangers and Auntie's regal acceptance of it were distasteful to her niece, who didn't hesitate to tell her so.

Philip Sears was introduced to Wo Peen at the dedication of the museum wing, and the young Indian consented to sit for a work to be entitled the *Dreamer*, a statue which would be the equal of *Pumunangwet* in physical beauty and which would symbolize contemplation as a complement to aspiration. Again, it was not commissioned by Miss Sears, but she purchased it several years after its completion, and its unveiling revealed her at her most testy. With her own household help assisting the caterer, Foster, who arrived with "twelve waiters, two cooks, one scullery maid," there were twenty-one altogether in the kitchen. After the coffee was passed, she rose imperiously and clapped her hands to command the attention of her luncheon guests. She then made a short speech and read the invocation, which Chief Bear Heart later sang in the Sioux language at the base of the statue. She took it for granted that her guests knew she had written it and was therefore much annoyed when she discovered that many were unaware of her authorship. Those who did know "took pains to go around and set [the others] straight on that subject."

A belated irritation further marred the memory of the occasion when two news articles stated that the *Dreamer* represented young Chief Metacom, called King Philip, hero of Miss Sears' *The Great Powwow*. One reporter asserted that the statue "symbolized the youthful King Philip.... It is an easy, seated pose - watchful and gazing silently into the distance - as Philip might have looked, seated on a boulder near the top of Mt. Wachusett, which was his headquarters." The article was well meant but facts were facts, and Clara Sears could brook no distortion.

Metacom was the son of the Wampanoag chief, Massasoit, friend and advisor of the early Cape Cod settlers. As Miss Sears wrote in *The Great Powwow*, Massasoit "did not live to see the day when the attitude of the white man became wholly that of a conqueror instead of that of a neighbor." Upon the death of his father, Metacom and his brother, Wamsutta, went to the authorities to receive English names, "in order to show their goodwill." Their regal bearing was so unmistakable that the names of the ancient Macedonian heros, Philip and Alexander, were bestowed upon them. It was Philip who saw fully that his race was doomed, and it was he who foresightedly organized an unprecedented confederation to defend Indian lands against the grasping English.

Forty-five years earlier, in 1629, Governor Endicott was doing his best to compensate the Indians for their land in accordance with his instructions from the Massachusetts Bay Company. Although John Endicott was scrupulous in the dealings over which he had control, the territory under his jurisdiction did not include all of what is now New England. Furthermore, as Endicott wrote home to England, it was becoming impossible to control "profane and dissolute" traders who defied the law by selling both guns and spirits to the Indians. Weapons armed them against the white men; liquor inflamed them. As Endicott's seven times great-granddaughter put it, "How the white man could have been so short-sighted as to furnish the Indians with a weapon which could so easily be used for his own destruction is a mystery hard to fathom.... The truth was that a great number of furs could be bought for a gun, and the spirit of greed overwhelmed the fear of future possibilities." In any case, the "easy conditions," the few coats and baubles paid to "avoyde the least scruple of intrusion," hastened white takeover of Indian lands.

Miss Sears was ahead of her time in understanding the complexities of Native Americans. She admired their affinity with nature and understood the frenzy which was excited by chiefs and medicine men in anticipation of battle. She felt, however, that the pagan mixture of sensitivity and ignorance was too complex for the settlers to fathom. "For with all their sterling qualities they were not endowed with an imagination of a kind to dissect such strange mental processes. Anything out of the ordinary they attributed to heathenism and the mechanisms of the Devil, and as everything seemed out of the ordinary to them regarding Indians, they assumed they were all devils, and that ended the matter for them."

King Philip tried to sustain the focus of his unlikely confederation, calling incompatible chiefs together for a great powwow on Mt. Wachusett, in 1675. Though "the cause was hopeless from the start," Miss Sears felt it was "none the less worthy in conception," and concluded that in the history of our country Metacom's name "must be found on the list of Patriots who gave their lives for an ideal."

By the time she wrote *The Great Powwow*, Clara Sears was certain of her ability to write important books about Nashua Valley idealists, but a new uncertainty surfaced. Would a book more sympathetic to Massachusetts Indians than to early colonists be readily accepted? Her Line-A-Day entry for July 14, 1933, when she received a positive letter from Houghton Mifflin, is girlishly enthusiastic. "I got a thrill for I did not feel sure how that kind of a book would appeal to them. So that's off my mind and I am happy about it." She immediately sent the news to her fellow authors, and Emilie Loring replied from Maine that it was a pity she was not nearer so they could "throw one wild party." It is difficult to envision what might have represented a wild party; Clara Sears did not imbibe although she offered cocktails to guests in proof of her modernity. The two women, nonetheless, looked forward to a celebration upon the book's publication and agreed that a great load had dropped from Clara's shoulders.

The *New York Times* praised her as a "sound, dependable writer on historic matters," one who filled her chapters "with authentic and colorful detail and human interest" and was uniquely "open-minded and just." Miss Sears sent the equally flattering *New York Herald Tribune* review to Virginia Ellis, who had become friend as much as secretary during the writing of *The Great Powwow*. Virginia's reply reflected the prevailing Bostonian annoyance with New Yorkers. She was

> glad to note that they have so truly measured the merit of the book. It must be very gratifying to have shown the New York people that Boston can produce works of art equal to their own very best, for as you have often said they are not as a rule over-friendly to Boston authors. And to have thus tamed the *Tribune* critics whom I have always understood to be unusually severe in their reviews is an accomplishment in itself. I can only say that reading these words of praise makes me still more proud of my association with "The Great Powwow" and above all with its author.

Clara Sears turned seventy in 1933, the year in which she completed this "great saga, as vivid as any novel." Professionally, the decade of the thirties was her Indian phase; personally, it was a period of recuperation and regeneration. Her spirits revived, and she settled down to reap the rewards of past ventures and to press onward with new projects. More relaxed herself, she turned her attention to the comfort of museum visitors and opened a tea room so that they could linger as long as they liked, all day if they wished, without having to interrupt their enjoyment of the buildings, the grounds, and the view. Miss Sears wanted her "guests" to be able to relax and absorb the peace of the scene and was determined "never to allow the place to become vulgarised." She insisted that it must not resemble public parks with "their swings and their tilting boards and their merry-go-rounds and a general appearance of holiday relaxation." It must always be a place of inspiration, not recreation, "a place where thinkers can come and find an atmosphere that is appealing to them." She was anxious to encourage visitors from all walks of life. As she told her trustees in 1939, "Even a policeman stuck his head through the window of my motor while I was waiting outside a store to tell me that he and his wife and children always made a pilgrimage to

Harvard each summer to spend a day on the Museum grounds. As he expressed it, 'They are swell!' What better tribute could one ask for?"

Although two art galleries and four more books were in the offing, Clara Sears, at eighty, became less obsessed with perfection and could turn the inevitable hitches in her projects to amusing account in the telling. With longevity a family precedent, she did not doubt but that she, too, had many years of productive life ahead of her. Having already accomplished a great deal, she allowed herself to pursue new goals with somewhat less intensity.

125

Chapter 9

Golden Hour

You came, - and then
Before we knew it
You had flown!-
Where to?
Far off, - to those unknown
Vast tractless realms
Called Memory!

Clara Endicott Sears

When Miss Sears was chauffeured on her errands around Harvard, the impression made upon townspeople was much as it had been when her mother was still alive. Miriam Shaw's figure, grown ample with the years, resembled that of Mrs. Sears, and the inevitable hats worn by the pair furthered the similarity. The two women lived near one another in both Harvard and Boston and shared many aspects of their single lives. When they took their accustomed seats at Symphony Hall for Friday afternoon performances during the winter, Miss Sears was often pointed out as an attraction in her own right. Just as at Fruitlands, however, Miriam frowned upon excessive lionizing of her aunt.

126

Cousin Fanny Mason often joined Miss Sears and her niece at musical events. By the age of eighty, Clara Sears could relax in the company of fond relatives and sincere friends. With a confidence achieved through success, she even rediscovered the light narrative touch of her 1895 European journal. She particularly liked to enliven annual reports to her trustees. When an infestation of termites was discovered at the Fruitlands farmhouse in 1938, she turned the frustrations of the actuality into dramatic merriment for their enjoyment. Her grounds keeper, Mr. Merrill, was "a man with a very dramatic soul," who had "a way of staring his eyes that makes one realize to the full all the darkest side of what has happened." The tale, as she told it, was more about the man than the infestation.

I realized all the horrors of the situation from his appearance. The men who were present at the time he made the discovery of the termites told me afterwards that he shouted "termites!" and ran around in circles jumping into the air! As to whether this was an expression of joy at finding a job which would have to be attended to or whether it was an expression of horror I leave to others to decide, keeping my own views to myself.

Mr. Merrill said he and his men could do the job perfectly well and that it would cost much less if they did it rather than getting some of those experts up here, and that assertion carried weight in my mind.... I came to Harvard almost every other day to overlook the work. I felt some qualms about his doing it but at the time it seemed the best way to do. I little realized the dramatic attitude Mr. Merrill would take in regard to the work. I supposed he would oversee the work but he said "no" he was going to do some of it himself as he needed the money, and he might as well get it as another man, so when I went there the first time when they were starting in I found him all arrayed in overalls, ready for the fray. He showed himself to me, turning himself back and front and I made out as best I could that I was duly impressed.... Next time I went up there Mr. Merrill came up from the cellar, with overalls torn, face covered with paint and breathing heavily as though he was working so

127

hard that he had thrown appearances to the winds. I saw that the other men were working along systematically, making no such fuss.... As I remained obdurate and would not be impressed Mr. Merrill took another tack. He asked me if I had noticed the color of his face. He said that it was growing yellow from the poison, and that he had been obliged to go to the doctor as he had been taken with violent cramps and the doctor had given him some medicine to counteract the cramps. I said, "Mr. Merrill, I never asked you to do this work. It is your own affair doing it. You said you wanted to. You ought never to have undertaken it if it was going to affect you so strangely, and I must ask you not to attempt any more of it." At that he changed the subject, and I went down into the cellar to see how the work was progressing. I did not suppose such an upheaval of everything was necessary, but Mr. Merrill said it was. The house had been jacked up and a layer of copper put between it and the foundations.... The cellar ground had to be dug down four feet and that same amount of fresh gravel put down to replace it. Twenty gallons of poison were sprayed into every crevice and over the gravel on the ground. Creosote was painted over everything and all around the windows.... It was certainly a job, but the other men seemed to take it quietly and were none the worse for the poison.

The next time I went up I found him wedged into a partition hard at work.... He was so busy he could hardly say good morning, but finally made the remark that he had gotten in there but he doubted very much whether he could get out! I asked him what could be done about it, and he replied that he didn't know, that his legs were getting very stiff and he felt as if they were swelling. It sounded bad. I suggested that the men might drag him out and that it had better be done at once before he swelled any more. I had visions of him swelling up so big that perhaps the partition would have to be cut away so as to extricate him. Something called me outside the house and soon he appeared with his eyes rolling. "You must excuse my hair," he said. I looked at it in alarm. "What's the matter with your hair?" I asked with concern. "Don't you see?" he replied. "It's turned all streaked and yellow from the poison." "Mr. Merrill," I said, with some impatience, "I cannot take the responsibility for

128

your continuing with this work. If it affects you so much that you have cramps, and your legs swell, and your hair is streaked with yellow, I cannot undertake to agree to your doing any more of it. I'd be much obliged if you discontinued it." Again he changed the subject quickly. It got so that I actually dreaded going up there, not knowing what condition I would find him in. Finally, after every organ in his body seemed to be in a state of revolt from the work, his imagination grew dim and he began on another tack.

Towards the ending of the work which had lasted about a month I went up there one day, and happily anticipating the finishing up of the job, I approached the old house and he came hurrying toward me. "How is everything?" I asked cheerfully yet with an inward feeling of misgiving. He began to stare his eyes ominously, and rolled them. "What is it, Mr. Merrill? What has happened?" I cried with a sudden fear. "Tell me, don't keep me waiting." His face grew very long. "It's the woodpeckers," he said in a whisper. "The woodpeckers!" I exclaimed. "For pity sake, what is the matter with the woodpeckers?"

I was exasperated. I felt as though I could not undertake to cope with woodpeckers after all I had had to do. "They've bored holes in the side of the water tank," he explained, "and have fallen in. The tank is full of drowned woodpeckers. You'll have to have a new tank!" "Indeed I'll do no such thing. Clean out the woodpeckers and empty out the water and air it out and let it go at that!" I was really annoyed at his suggestion of a new tank. The water in that tank was only used in case of fire. It is not meant to drink. A few woodpeckers more or less would not hurt it. Mr. Merrill saw that I was annoyed and out of patience, so he said no more on that subject, but he gave me the unpleasant news that the termite work had amounted to a good deal more than he thought it would, but it could not be helped. I made up my mind then and there that I would never again have a piece of work like that done by anyone but experts, and I have since found out that the experts would have done it for less than half the price that Mr. Merrill charged.

I could not resist giving a detailed account of my experiences with the termites, but I would not wish to do Mr. Merrill harm by so doing. Mr. Merrill is a very pleasant man and under him his men do beautiful work as a rule.

No sooner had Fruitlands been saved from the termites (actually powderpost beetles) than Miss Sears began to make inquiries as to local talent available for the construction of a picture gallery she had designed to house her burgeoning collection of primitive American portraits. She had been gathering the work of itinerant painters for quite some time and now, she decided, she had enough to share with the public. Although she claimed simply to have drifted into the desire to collect the works of these nineteenth century artists, one portrait leading to another, they were actually of particular interest to her, having been painted during the period when Bronson Alcott was at Fruitlands, when the Shakers were in the middle of their great revival, and while William Miller was prophesying the end of the world.

In the course of collecting Indian artifacts, Miss Sears had "formed the habit of stopping at the door of the lovely old farm houses that dot the countryside and chatting with the owners." She now continued the practice, inducing the owners "to bring from the attic whatever old portraits they had for me to see." Her visits were less random, however, for she placed notices in newspapers and methodically verified all responses concerning artists as well as sitters. She prided herself on not delegating this research to others, remarking proudly, "I did it myself." Every minute thus spent was a great pleasure to her. She often spoke of the enjoyment she found in sitting on countless cracker barrels and soap boxes, "listening to the old people relate things of long ago."

Miss Sears' interest continued to center on personalities, as a Boston reporter noted when she brought forty-one of her paintings to Doll and Richards for the city's first comprehensive exhibit of primitives. Moving from portrait to portrait, she explained the personalities of the sitters "as if they were her intimates." In some instances, such was indeed the case, at least in a historical sense. She had been able, for example, to purchase the likenesses of a young couple from a woman who had inherited the paintings but had no room to hang them. The groom, Jonathan Wheeler, was "a most extraordinarily good looking young man with a high stock on and a velvet collar to his coat, and what was even more appealing, - the suggestion of a dimple in his cheek and a very decided lilt in his eye." The bride-to-be, Elizabeth Davenport, had her hair piled up startlingly high on her head in curls and braids, but hers was a "New England face with conscientious scruples written all over it." Miss Sears could be sure of her observation because with the paintings she also acquired a little trunk containing the love letters of the two, "demure beyond anything," and inexpressibly touching to the author of three romantic novels with similarly chaste heroines. It was with great hesitation that she opened the letters, feeling "almost ashamed" to intrude upon the couple's privacy though their love story was over a hundred years old. The young bride died within a year of her marriage, and Miss Sears found in the trunk with the letters "a little purse containing a few cents, and to it was tied a strip of paper on which was written, 'This is my beloved's purse just as she left it. I shall follow her soon.' " He did not, of course, but the sentiment was of exactly the romantic sort to touch Clara Sears, who liked to think, "there always remained in his heart a certain secret place where little Elizabeth Davenport, his first love, held sway for always."

Miss Sears opened her gallery in Harvard in June of 1940 and published *Some American Primitives* in 1941. The book was amply illustrated and anecdotal in character, full of stories about sitters and artists alike. She made no claim to having written a definitive work but succeeded in her plan to furnish examples of primitive portraiture, signed and unsigned, beginning with "real primitives" and developing from that point to "the gradations of talent that led some of the itinerant portrait painters to develop into artists of note, and in a few cases of international fame." In

131

this sense she knew she was doing "pioneer work," but her great-
est personal pleasure continued to come from the stories told her
about the artists and the sitters. As the *New York Tribune*
reviewer expressed it, "Doubtless what would please her most in
response to her book would be additional information about these
itinerant artists."

In tracking down the artist who painted the unsigned portrait
of a young girl called Lottie Reed, Miss Sears discovered the work
of Jones Fawson Morris, who "had a way of over-consoling himself
when he was about to paint a portrait," requiring a state of inebri-
ation in order to complete the work. With evident delight she
recounted the following story of a mother's concern as Mr. Morris
took the likenesses of her three children.

> She had heard rumors that he had a very unfortunate
> trick of consoling himself at times by taking a drop too
> much, but she did not know if it was true or not. So it was
> arranged that he should come on a certain day, and when
> the day came she dressed the three children in their Sunday
> suits and washed their faces and smoothed their hair, and
> they sat waiting for the artist to come. He appeared at the
> foot of the walk leading to the front door. Mrs. Dix watched
> him critically as he approached to see if he walked all right.
> Something made her nervous as she looked at his legs but
> she thought it might be her imagination, and she ushered
> him into the best parlor where the painting was to be done.
> All went well except that instead of posing the children as
> she supposed he would with their arms entwined, one hold-
> ing a bird cage and another a toy whip, he stood them up in
> a row just as they were which rather disappointed her. The
> next day he came again and finished all but the eyes which
> he told her he always left to the final sitting, and he said he
> would come the next day and paint them in. When the next
> day came she and the children were sitting waiting for him
> near the front door which was open. When she saw him
> appear her heart misgave her. As he came up the path lead-
> ing to the house she saw that his legs were distinctly wobbly
> and she quickly shooed the children into the best parlor. He
> came into the house and trembling with fear and indignation

she told him to go home as he was not in a fit condition to do any painting on the children's portrait to say nothing of painting in the eyes. He was most cheerful and casual about it, and told her that it was necessary that she should give him some more drink. She did not know what to do, and being rather afraid of him she went down cellar and came up with a tumbler full. He drank it down at a gulp. Then before she could prevent him he turned and went into the best parlor where the children were. She rushed forward saying that she refused to allow him to attempt the painting of her children's eyes, and for him to get up and go home.

He took this perfectly cheerfully and said, "Don't you mind a bit now. I don't and if I don't why should you?" and he told her to take the portrait off of the easel and prop it up against something steady, and to bring him his pallet and brushes and he could paint in the eyes all right sitting on the floor. Poor Mrs. Dix, she was in a dilemma, she did not know what to do, but he insisted, so she took the portrait down from the easel and propped it against the best black hair cloth sofa and gave him his pallet and brushes. Then she sank into a rocking chair awaiting the worst, while she covered her face with her hand. She could hear him puffing and blowing and it sounded as if he were sort of tumbling about trying to steady himself. Her curiosity got the better of her and she peeked through her fingers to see what was going on. To her terror she saw him wielding his paint brush high in the air in a most inconsequent manner, swooping down onto the canvass in a hit or miss fashion. In her mind's eye she saw her poor children going down to posterity depicted as being wall-eyed, squint-eyed, pop-eyed, heaven knows what, and she sank back in the rocking chair again, exhausted. After this had gone on for some time she heard him give a final puff and she opened her eyes again, and heard him mutter that the portrait was finished. She braced herself to see something terrible. Instead, to her amazement she saw three pairs of blue eyes looking straight out from the canvass resembling perfectly those of her children!

Having frequently sat for portraits, Miss Sears was familiar with the eccentricities of artists and was not unaware that her eyes were among her most striking features. Paintings and photographs of her, from the 1870 portrait by George Southward onward, show a pensive yet intense gaze. When Alfred Jonniaux painted her in 1949 he said, "Everything must be concentrated on your face and your sparkling eyes through which I hope to achieve the portrait of your spirit!" At nearly eighty-seven, that spirit remained indomitable.

Miss Sears designed a special alcove for the Jonniaux in the foyer of the Portrait Gallery and sometimes sat by the painting to greet visitors. Having two Clara Endicott Searses in the same small anteroom seemed almost overpowering. When, for a time, the portrait was hung in the tea room, the attention of luncheon guests was immediately attracted by the elegance of her pink gown and her pearls and by the attractive tilt of her wide-brimmed black hat; but they left with the memory that wherever they went in the room, Miss Sears' eyes appeared to be following them with curiosity and interest. Neither in life nor in the portrait did she look her years, and for once the press was not exaggerating when a reporter from the *Boston Post* described her as "slim, small and incredibly chic, with a figure and posture that would make a young woman envious."

By this time, she had received many honors. Her biography was included in *Leading Women of America*, and she had been elected to the National Institute of Social Sciences. She was honorary president of the Boston branch of the National League of American Penwomen and an honorary member of the Professional Women's Club. In 1942 she was invited to Cleveland to accept the medal of honor of the National Society of New England Women. Having become more than content to remain in her own "little corner of New England," she was at first "appalled" at the thought of such a journey; but when she heard that Henry Ford and Van Wyck Brooks had received the same medal, she realized that she "was indeed in good company" and "became quite thrilled at the thought of going." That Miriam Shaw asked to go along "was an added joy," and on May 16 the two set off on the night train from Worcester. After a prearranged day's rest, they presented themselves at the head table for the May 18 luncheon ceremony. Ever susceptible to sentiment and praise, Miss Sears found it an emotional occasion, so moving that she declined to remain for the evening's speeches and festivities, giving as an excuse the fact of train reservations. However, as she told her trustees, "My very real reason for not doing so was that I thought it would seem like an anti-climax." She wanted to keep the group's warm reception and her own exhilaration in mind "and not have any of the edge taken off" by lingering on.

The caliber and sincerity of the women had touched her, and a closing rendition of "The Unfurling of the Flag" had left her in a state of personal and patriotic upheaval. World War II was very much on all minds at the time. As she said afterward to Miriam, "I don't think we need worry about this country with women like that in it." She treasured the society's gold medal, with a scene of the Pilgrims landing at Plymouth, and framed the accompanying citation.

> We take unusual pleasure in honoring you as a true daughter of New England by your ancestry, your place of residence, your projects carried on, your books written and by your outlook on life. You are known as a delver into the past, a lover of all things beautiful, and a collector in the best sense of the word. You love beauty and the ideals and history of New England, you believe in spiritual values. You have tried to help people appreciate the influences of this country in a way that will lead them to preserve our priceless heritage.

Two months after the excitement of her reception at Cleveland, Miss Sears had a fall that resulted in a broken nose and, ironically, more admiration. She took the accident so calmly that her equanimity was much remarked upon, prompting Miriam to write, "I was very proud to belong to you! When I tell people about your fall and the broken nose, they all say, 'Isn't she marvelous!' and I say, 'Yes, she certainly is!' "

Miriam and Miss Sears had to curtail their drives about the countryside as a result of gas rationing during World War II. The war also deprived Miss Sears of the services and companionship of Virginia Ellis, who was stationed in England with the American Red Cross. Miss Sears was a better correspondent than Virginia, keeping her up to date with a barrage of news clippings about Harvard and Boston events. Virginia felt somewhat hampered in writing because of wartime censorship but was free to indulge in a touch of nostalgia. "You will be getting ready for Harvard and the Museums' opening pretty soon, and I wish I could be there to help. But, I am very happy here and am still sure I have done the right thing. Do write me occasionally and remember that I think often of the fun it was to be with you and how very good you have always been to me."

Virginia also sent news about Mary Carnegie, who remained in England even after the death of her second husband in 1936. She lived in a badly bombed neighborhood of London, "surrounded by shells of houses," but refused to abandon the city, preferring to take the war in stride and turn the days of the blitz into amusing stories. "Nothing, apparently, can frighten her," wrote Virginia. In tribute to the "courage and fortitude with which she is facing the horror that confronts all her country," Mary Carnegie's nearest relatives in the United States contributed a fully equipped ambulance to the British Expeditionary force, which had lost all of its own in Flanders. Miss Sears contributed five hundred dollars and soon after received "a knockout blow" that brought the fact of war too close to home. Camp Devens, across the Nashua River from the Pergolas, had become Fort Devens, and she was required to turn over to it two hundred acres of land, including the Sacred Grove of the Alcotts, where the transcendentalists had mused on matters of deep philosophy. "Sentiment could not enter into governmental plans," she lamented, "so there was nothing left for me to do but let it go."

Reluctantly, she was obliged to enforce a wartime restriction of her own. Although she decided to keep the museums open in order to offer the public some small respite from the cares of the war, she had to close the tea room because of rationing and the scarcity of help. Hoping that a few would find their way to the museums' "atmosphere of peace," she was quite surprised when many did so. "Being very much curtailed myself I marveled when I saw motors sailing down the hill to Fruitlands with perfect ease of conscience and velocity. We did not make it our business to penetrate their methods of getting sufficient gas, but were glad, if they were bound on going somewhere, that they chose this place to come to."

Before the 1942 closing of the tea room, military families from Fort Devens often relaxed in its atmosphere, but when an old army horse galloped onto the scene Miss Sears had fodder for a raucous tale for her trustees.

> When making my rounds of the place I saw a most dilapidated horse grazing in the field next to the farm barn. I asked the farmer, Mudgett, who it belonged to. He said it was one he had hired to help in the haying. He admitted it was a queer looking horse, and that its knees were spavined, but it was the only one he could get, for Fort Devens was picking up all the horses in the neighborhood. I looked at it dubiously in the light of a help in haying, but I made no further comment.
>
> A few hours later the Tea Room was very busy with guests. A number of officers and their wives and families had turned up for lunch, besides other parties, and the tables inside the Tea Room, and on the terrace, as well as those in the arbor, were full.
>
> Suddenly a bugle was heard blowing from the Fort, and at the same time three officers on thoroughbred horses came galloping across the fields to get to the road, and coming to

the enclosure where the old horse was grazing, which was fenced in, they took a flying jump, clearing the fence and landing out in the road.

When the old horse heard the bugle he became transformed. He threw his head back, whisked his tail, and started to run around his paddock, and when the officers jumped into his domain and rushed past him onto the road, his exhilaration knew no bounds. He gathered himself together, took a run, and made for the fence at full tilt, and up he went, and landed on the other side! He staggered a little, when he got there, but his spirit was good, and finding himself free, in pure joy he galloped down the road, turned into the Museums avenue and plunged right up onto the terrace where the guests were having lunch! It was an overwhelming moment! Seeing a loose horse coming right towards them caused a dire confusion to reign. Some of the women screamed. There was general springing up from the tables, and one and all made for the door of the Tea Room, and pushed their way in tumultuously, and the people lunching in the Arbor did likewise. Mrs. Sawyer, who runs the Tea Room, ran to the door and waved a large towel frantically in front of the horse. This he took great exception to, and giving one final kick-up with his legs to show it, he galloped off the terrace onto the avenue, rather the worse for wear, but still game.

We had to get rid of him. He agitated us too much. It turned out that he was an old army horse, and the sound of the bugle went like wine to his head.

It was hard to believe that Miss Sears had not yet done with creating new museums, but at the trustees' meeting of 1945 she called their attention to the fact that she had for some time been collecting paintings of Hudson River School artists, beginning with an Alvan Fisher inherited from her Sears grandfather. She was now "exceedingly anxious" to round out her plant by adding an ell onto the Picture Gallery. "If I can finish out my dream, I shall indeed be a happy woman." She wanted to exhibit these uniquely American landscapes depicting the rough beauty of a nation seeking its manifest destiny, many of which had transcendental overtones.

The construction of her ell was not easily accomplished. The original builder dragged his feet, and when Miss Sears hired a new one, rain, snow, and sleet impeded progress. Fortunately, foresight on her part resulted in the purchase of girders before the imposition of a wartime ban on the sale of steel; but, in general, she wrote,

> 1946 has proved itself no better than 1945. That is a rather dismal conclusion to come to, but it is only the truth. Last year we were buoyed up by the conviction that help would be plentiful, food would be plentiful, stores would hold all the things necessary to civilized living, - in fact the old world would return to pre-war standards, and we would all be happy again, in 1946. It was a Utopian dream...as crazy a dream of Utopia as the one Bronson Alcott dreamed when he led the ox-cart that held all his furniture through the tumble-down gate at Fruitlands in 1843. But that dream of his contained waves of the Spirit - this wave through which we are passing is a wholly material one, which makes it worse.

The museum became a reality nonetheless, and Miss Sears published *Highlights among the Hudson River Artists* soon thereafter. The book made no pretensions to being learned but was very much on the pattern of *Some American Primitives*, "assembled in a human sort of way," full of quotations from the artists, and illustrated by paintings from her own collection. Again, she relied professionally on the advice of experts, this time from Boston's Vose Gallery. Wrote Robert Vose in 1959, the year before her death, "In the good old days, when you were planning the magnificent collection you have formed - year after year you came here the first day of the exhibition, selected about three of the best pictures, bought them and put them in storage. Then Mrs. Vose and I went for your opening exhibition, and what a thrill it was to me to see the proportion of the more important pictures which had come from us."

Each of the artists included in her book emerged "as a personality." It would have surprised her to know it, but she had effectively masked her own personality to the extent that those describing her dealt in stereotypical generalities. She was seen as an aloof and demanding aristocrat. As her estate superintendent remarked, "I don't know whether you would call her impressive or dignified, but you didn't take liberties with her." She mistakenly prided herself on being approachable and confided to a reporter, "I shop everywhere for my clothes, yes, in the downtown department stores as well as in the smaller shops, wherever the fancy strikes me, wherever I see something that appeals to me. And all the girls know me and call me 'dear.' " That the shop girls called her "dear" did not make them her intimates, nor would she have wanted any such thing. In reality, she was more comfortable with them than they with her, as she encouraged them to chat about themselves. She felt it a great pity that so few people took time to listen, "for the woman who listens and remembers becomes a very interesting person as she grows older." She knew she had fine-honed her story-telling talents and was sought after as a lively raconteuse.

Sara Ware Bassett was not quite so liberal minded about familiar verbal exchanges with the younger generation, or with her elders for that matter. After more than forty years' friendship with Clara, she continued to address her friend as Miss Sears. Miss Bassett tried to adapt herself to changing times and "bump along over the jolts," but, she said, "when the sprightly young waitresses at the [Authors'] Club shout 'Hi, Miss Bassett,' I nod cheerfully and politely but I cannot bring myself to shout back 'Hi!' As for the clothes - or lack of them - well, enough said."

The two women exchanged observations and accepted the physical limitations of aging, but their group was narrowing, "and those who are left are the dearer to one another." When Emilie Loring died in 1951, her son wrote Miss Sears, "Your friendship was one of the shining points in her life and I thank you from the bottom of my heart for being so wonderful to her." Mrs. Loring was missed at the Athenaeum, but Miss Bassett and Miss Sears continued to write there, glad not to "let our old and precious friendship pass without little glimpses of one another now and then." They also visited occasionally during the summer months, driving back and forth between their summer homes, across the Nashua Valley from one another. Miss Bassett wrote in 1954, when she was eighty-one and Miss Sears was ninety-one, "I do not mean to slump back into an idle old age. You never will and I don't mean to."

In the spring of that year, Miss Sears received an honor which was undoubtedly initiated on her behalf and which gave her immense gratification, The First Annual Authors' Club's Citation of Distinction. Miss Bassett was happy for her and wrote, "I cannot tell you how delighted I am that the first award of the Authors' Club should have gone to you, who so richly deserve it.... You carried it off beautifully." The following year Miss Bassett received the award herself, and those present thought they had never seen her quite so happy. The two continued their writing, undaunted by age, though Miss Bassett, because of the severe illness of her sister in 1957, wrote to say, "My writing career is definitely over and the Athenaeum sees me no more. I thought I would tell you this as perhaps you did not know that I had 'graduated.' "

Miss Sears, who had by no means put aside her own typewriter, now wintered at the hotel that had so intrigued her in her youth, the Vendome. She turned her two-room suite into a summer-like haven with furniture painted pale green, flowered wallpaper, and ferns in the bay window. At Christmas time, poinsettias replaced potted gardenias, and her retired chauffeur,

Sharples, made it his annual practice to bring her a gift of holiday cookies. Though he never overstepped his bounds, he knew his employer as well as anyone. He had driven her for nearly thirty years, ever since the days when she arrived unannounced in farmyards, asking for "strange looking stones." He had been witness to the spontaneity of her excitements and disappointments, and he had an immense respect for her. It was evidence of his affection, as well, that he refused to let the 1957 holiday season pass by without his Christmas visit although he had been very ill after a heart attack. As his daughter wrote Miss Sears, "Father continues to improve, and you may be interested to know that he insisted on driving in with me on Christmas Day to deliver your cookies. It was his first trip out, and he was very shaky on his feet - but he seemed to want to do everything as he always had. He took the basket into the hotel alone and I rejoiced that he was able to do so - even if he cannot do very much more than that."

The previous winter, when Miss Sears was ninety-three, she wrote Miss Bassett that she was conserving her own strength for finishing *Early Personal Reminiscences*. She had had the memoir in mind for some time and had begun snatches even before Virginia Ellis went off to war more than a decade earlier. By the time of the book's publication, Dr. Ellis had died and Virginia wrote to say, "I think only of you and our happy relationship and also of my good father who did bring us together. I can remember so well the days of your planning it, and I am proud...that I may have typed one of the rough drafts of the first chapter...ours is a long association which I treasure tremendously."

Clara Endicott Sears had a final visit with her cousin, Mary Endicott Chamberlain Carnegie, who in 1955 crossed the Atlantic all alone on the *Queen Elizabeth*, on seas so rough that she felt as though the ocean liner were but a "cockle shell." "All through our growing up," Clara recalled in *Early Personal Reminiscences*, "she and I were like sisters, and that precious and close intimacy has continued up to this day." Mrs. Carnegie was still remembered by some in England as "the little Puritan," although Queen Victoria had given her a gold medal and King George VI had offered her a peerage. On her side of the Atlantic, the aristocratic Clara once laughingly remarked, "People say that I am the Queen Mary of Boston." Together for the last time after almost a century of lives fully lived, Mary and Clara savored memories of their childhood and decided that the memoir in preparation should include an account of their early effort to bring a touch of royalty to Salem.

We decided to do something to bring a glimpse of royalty into the streets of Salem. The more we thought of it the better we liked it. It was to be like a King and Queen Act, so to speak. Mary was to take the part of the king, while I by preference, was to be the queen, because I shrank with all my soul from putting on trousers. Mary had no sensitive feelings on the subject, having a big brother, and so accepted the situation.

At the first opportunity she went to William's closet to choose her apparel, from which she emerged swallowed up in a pair of discarded trousers that were so big and so loose that she had all the appearance of a miniature old-clothes-man. Topping this was a most disreputable and moth-eaten coat, and, as a finishing touch, a strange looking article, which we had fashioned in gold paper to look like a crown, perched on the top of her head.

After searching in the garret I discovered a worn-out dress with a long train which seemed to me to be eminently fitting. This I put on me, the volume of which practically hid me from sight. Wrapped in an old shawl and with an equally strange erection for a crown on my head, I joined Mary.

For a moment we looked at each other critically, then instantly agreed there was something radically lacking in or appearance - we did not look sufficiently royal. Then of a sudden an inspiration came. Mary seized a downy feather cushion off the sofa and pinned it over her stomach and tucked it inside the voluminous trousers, while declaring that she had heard somewhere that all kings had protruding stomachs. And I, hearing this, seized another downy cushion and pinned it behind on my back like a bustle, believing it would give a royal look to my outfit.

Thus equipped, Mary stood up so straight that she almost bent backwards, and I bent forward, and apparently satisfied with ourselves we strode out of the house, arm in arm, and emerged onto Essex Street, with the congratulations of Martha Dempsey, the Endicotts' faithful housemaid of long standing, who watched us go on our way.

A good many of those passing along the street looked at us with extreme amusement as well as amazement which we thought was admiration. I said triumphantly to Mary, "I guess now we look royal all right."

When Mary died in London, in May of 1957, Miriam was a comfort to her aunt, and Miss Bassett was "glad that you have her near you now," but Miss Sears was struck by the realization that there was no one left to call her Clara. Three years later she died peacefully at the Vendome on March 25, 1960, having lived her life "exactly as I would have ordered it, had such a thing been possible." An article in the *New York Sun* once observed

Clara Endicott Sears seems to regard the past as having been lived chiefly for the benefit of the future. The present she regards as a convenient work season arranged for her by Father Time in which she can make the future still more aware of the past.

Upon her death, she did indeed leave the preservation of the past as her legacy to the future.

Bibliography

Notes

Acknowledgments

Index

Bibliography

Alcott, Bronson. "Diary, 1841," *The Dial*, II (April 1842).

Alcott, Bronson, and Charles Lane. "Fruitlands," *The Dial*, IV (July 1843).

Amory, Cleveland. *The Proper Bostonians*. New York: E.P. Dutton and Co., Inc., 1947.

Ashburn, Frank. *Peabody of Groton*. New York: Coward McCann, 1944.

Endicott, C.M. *A Genealogy of the Peabody Family*. Boston: by the author, 1867.

Endicott, William C. *John Endicott and John Winthrop*. Boston: by the author, 1930.

Endicott, William C. *Memoir of Samuel Endicott*. Boston: by the author, 1924.

Fruitlands Archives

Canning and Evaporating Club (booklet).

Corporation Records.

Journals:
Miss Sears, European trip, 1895.
Mrs. Sears, European trips, 1895, 1904, 1906.

Letters, bound by topic:
> Books by Clara Endicott Sears, I-VI.
> Colonel Welch and Fort Lapwai.
> Fruitlands, I-IV.
> Henry T, Newman, I-II.
> Indian Museum, I-II.
> Indians.
> Miscellaneous, I-III.
> Pergolas.
> War Time Canning Club and Camp Devens.

Letters, unbound.

Line-a-Day Diaries.

Scrapbooks:
> Clara Endicott Sears. (The abbreviation Scrap. in the notes refers to this scrapbook.)
> Mary Peabody Sears.
> George Peabody.

Speeches.

Grant, Robert. *Fourscore*. Boston: Houghton Mifflin, 1934.

Grant, Robert. *The North Shore of Massachusetts*. New York: Charles Scribner's Sons, 1896.

Harris, Ida A. *Harvard History 1894-1940*. Harvard, Massachusetts, Historical Society.

Lawrence, Ruth, editor. *Colonial Families of America*. New York: National Americana Society.

Morison, Samuel Eliot. *Builders of the Bay Colony*. Cambridge: The Riverside Press, Houghton Mifflin, 1930.

O'Brien, Harriet E. *Lost Utopias*. Harvard, MA: Fruitlands and the Wayside Museums, Inc., 1947.

Peabody, Selim H. *Peabody Genealogy*. Boston: Charles H. Pope, 1909.

BIBLIOGRAPHY

Powers, Edwin. *Crime and Punishment in Early Massachusetts 1620-1692.* Boston: Beacon Press, 1966.

Shepard, Odell. *Pedlar's Progress.* Boston: Little, Brown and Company, 1937.

Tharp, Louise Hall. *Mrs. Jack.* Boston: Little, Brown and Company, 1965.

Winthrop, John. *The History of New England from 1630 to 1649.* Edited by James Savage. Boston: Little, Brown and Company, 1853.

Winthrop, John. *Winthrop Papers.* Boston: The Massachusetts Historical Society, 1931.

Winthrop, Robert C. *Memoir of the Honorable David Sears.* Cambridge: Massachusetts Historical Society, 1886.

Young, Alexander. *Chronicles of the First Planters of the Colony of Massachusetts Bay from 1632-1636.* Reprint of 1846 volume. Williamstown, MA: Corner House Publishers, 1978.

Books by Clara Endicott Sears

Sears, C.E. *The Bell-Ringer.* Boston: Houghton Mifflin Company, 1918.

Sears, C.E. *Bronson Alcott's Fruitlands.* Boston: Houghton Mifflin Company, 1915.

Sears, C.E. *Days of Delusion.* Boston: Houghton Mifflin Company, 1924.

Sears, C.E. *Early Personal Reminiscences.* Concord, New Hampshire: by the Author, 1956.

Sears, C.E. *Gleanings from Old Shaker Journals.* Boston: Houghton Mifflin Company, 1916.

Sears, C.E. *The Great Powwow.* Boston: Houghton Mifflin Company, 1934.

Sears, C.E. *Highlights among the Hudson River Artists.* Boston: Houghton Mifflin Company, 1947.

Sears, C.E. *The Power Within.* Harvard, Mass.: by the author, 1911.

Sears, C.E. *The Romance of Fiddler's Green.* Boston: Houghton Mifflin Company, 1922.

Sears, C.E. *Selections from "Your Forces and How to Use Them."* Harvard, Mass: by the author, 1916.

Sears, C.E. *Snapshots from Old Registers.* Boston: by the author, 1955.

Sears, C.E. *Some American Primitives.* Boston: Houghton Mifflin Company, 1941.

Sears, C.E. *Whispering Pines.* Falmouth, Mass.: Enterprise Press, 1930.

Sears, C.E. *Wind from the Hills.* New York: G.P. Putnam's Sons, 1936.

Notes

Chapter 1

Early Personal Reminiscences, privately printed by Clara Sears in 1956, has been an invaluable resource. Beginning with walking the table at Thanksgiving, all references to her early Salem memories have been taken from that small volume, which is in the Fruitlands Archives.

1   "All honor, then": *Essex County Mercury*, September 25, 1878.

5   "unfit persons": Alexander Young, *Chronicles of the First Planters of the Colony of Massachusetts Bay from 1623-1636* (Williamstown, MA: Corner House Publishers, 1978. Reprint of Young's 1846 volume), pp. 195-196. These records of the Governor and Company of the Massachusetts Bay in New England noted from proceedings of the General Court, April 30, 1629, that the "Governor, or Deputy, and Council, or the greater number of them, at an ample Court assembled, shall have power, and hereby are authorized...to remove and displace such unfit person or persons...."

"subjection to ecclesiastical": Edwin Powers, *Crime and Punishment in Early Massachusetts 1620-1692* (Boston: Beacon Press, 1966), p. 102.

6   "because it represented": William C. Endicott, *John Endicott and John Winthrop* (Boston: by the author, 1930), p. 18.

"disabled for one year": John Winthrop, *The History of New England from 1630 to 1649*, 2 vols. (Boston: Little Brown, 1853, James Savage, editor), vol. 1, p. 189.

"Why on earth": William C. Endicott, *Memoir of Samuel Endicott* (Boston: by the author, 1924), p. 6.

7   "with the chauffeur group"... "couldn't be relegated": Museum Archives. (Materials referenced to Museum Archives are filed together at Fruitlands.) Kate Cotharin, corresponding secretary of the Massachusetts Indian Association, sent a letter to Miss Sears regarding preparations for the ceremony, which she was helping to coordinate. Miss Cotharin was aware of the potential difficulty and passed the problem on to Miss Sears, "who solves difficulties so easily." Miss Cotharin had already asked David not to wear his "lizard of beads" or his bow of pink chiffon. Although she appreciated the Indian "love of decoration," these items "fairly took away" her appetite when David wore them to the Republican Club.

Page

"considering the many": W.C. Endicott, *John Endicott and John Winthrop*, p. 24. The General Court did not recognize the initial grant by the Indians but acknowledged and carried out their intent by judging "meete to give (unto his sonne) fower hundred acres of land."

8   "his reputation was such": Frank Ashburn, *Peabody of Groton* (New York: Coward McCann, 1944), p. 6.

9   "I won't walk": Endicott, *Memoir of Samuel Endicott*, p. 25.

      "Later in life": Ibid., p. 26.

10   "Give out something": Scrap., p. 155, *Boston Transcript*, April 20, 1936.

Chapter 2

13   "Therefore lett us choose": Governor John Winthrop, *Winthrop Papers*, 5 vols. (Boston: Massachusetts Historical Society, 1931), vol. 2, p. 295.

      "little broccoli sprout": Sears, *Early Pers. Rem.*, p. 25.

14   "To the cemetery": Ibid., p. 22.

15   "But, Monsieur Marquis": Ibid., p. 37.

17   "a typical gentleman": *Colonial Families of America* (New York: National Americana Society, Ruth Lawrence, editor).

      "revealed the sporting spirit"... "a policeman": Scrap., p. 224, *Boston Sunday Post*, December 7, 1947.

19   "After a too copious"... "serious indigestion"... "There is but a step": Robert C. Winthrop, *Memoir of the Honorable David Sears* (Cambridge, MA: by the author, 1886), p. 6.

      officers in the Union army: Ibid., p. 16. These cousins were Lt. Colonel Caspar Crowninshield, Captain F. S. Grand-d'Hauteville, Lt. C. W. Amory.

      "had a sound": Scrap., p. 155, *Boston Transcript*, April 20, 1936.

20   "took off his hat": Ibid.

      "It is obvious": Winthrop, *Memoir of the Honorable David Sears*, p. 19.

21   "a frown": Ibid., p. 20.

      "quite a severe letter"... "this in some measure": Museum Archives. Letter from Roger L. Scaife of Harvard University Press, March 26, 1946.

22   "[my] husband had not seen": Sears, *Days of Delusion*, p. 188.

      "Their success": Ibid., p. 113.

23   "Mr. Peabody!": Ibid., p. 176.

      "Let him which": Ibid., p. 153.

25   "The dairy was run": *Early Pers. Rem.*, pp. 46-47.

NOTES

Chapter 3

Mrs. Sears' scrapbook is the source of information concerning the Boston and Washington events that took place during Judge Endicott's term as secretary of war. Unfortunately, she did not include the names of the newspapers with the clippings.

27 "a coy glance": *Early Pers. Rem.*, p. 15. On a childhood visit to Mary's, Clara came down with chicken pox and passed some time watching the scene that took place regularly of a Sunday afternoon, on Essex Street. Young men strolled down the street while young women strolled up it. As they passed, the men lifted their hats in unison while the girls bowed soberly and demurely. After their bows, some of the girls would "look back over their shoulders surreptitiously to see if the young men were looking round at them...." Then they all reversed direction, continuing the process the whole of the afternoon.

"September sunshine": *Whispering Pines*, p. 50.

29 "The Fatal Sisters": Museum Archives. The poem was hand written and signed by Robert Grant, September 1882, Nahant.

"The Legend of Swallows' Cave": Museum Archives.

30 "Vesper Bells": *Wind From the Hills*, p. 59.

31 "The good ladies"... "I don't know": *Snapshots from Old Registers*, pp. 170-171.

33 "I went to hear": Museum Archives.

"While Miss Clara Sears": Scrap., p. 218, *Boston Sunday Herald*, January 14, 1899.

35 She told an interviewer: Scrap., p. 155. *Boston Transcript*, April 20, 1936.

36 "do something more constructive": Ibid.

"too hardened": Museum Archives. The samaritan of the story was described by Miss Sears as "the plainest the Almighty ever made, it seemed to me. She was ill-shaped, and her hair was carroty red, and she had very long teeth, and big hands and feet. I used to look at her in wonder, and pity, for she was very fine in character, and it seemed to me a tragedy that anyone would have to go through life so handicapped. Her unselfishness was something to reverence. She never seemed to think of herself. It was always of others that she thought. And yet behind it all I used to imagine that she suffered because of her affliction, for one could only call it that. I knew she did, I did not only imagine it. I knew that it could not possibly be otherwise."

40 "our old original stock"... "home-like"... "Then it came over me": Museum Archives. Speech to the Massachusetts Society of Mayflower Descendants, June 9, 1934.

43 orchid: Mrs. Sears' Scrap. Joseph Chamberlain had two nicknames, Orchid Joe and Pushing Joe. "Pushing Joe describes the absolute 'cheek,' perseverance and industry of the politician who first applied the American caucus system to British elections, had himself elected Mayor of Birmingham, was elected to Parliament, and after only four years had a seat in the cabinet as colonial secretary. Orchid Joe has

reference to the fine man of pleasure and apparent leisure, who has one of the rarest collections of orchids in the world, and invariably wears one in his buttonhole, but who is as welcome in Belgravia drawing rooms and Marlborough House as in the slums of Birmingham."

Mary's traveling costume: Mrs. Sears' Scrap. Later, when Mary Chamberlain was presented to Queen Victoria, she received special permission to wear a gown cut in a V, front and back, rather than the required decollete in which "many another less beautiful woman shivered." In Mary's simple gown of brocaded white satin by Worth, "there was much to remind Americans present at the charmed court of the little Puritan bride in her simple wedding gown of gray cloth."

45   Felicia Dorothy Hemans, 1793-1835. "A Dirge."

      "In the death": Museum Archives.

46   "If I had emotional courage": *Early Pers. Rem.*, p. 65.

      "Was it Duty calling?": *Whispering Pines*, p. 65.

Chapter 4

All information and quotes concerning the European trips are from the journals kept at the time by Miss Sears or her mother. These diaries are now in the Museum Archives.

47   "It was this tendency": *Fiddler's Green*, p. 50.

48   "He walked about": *Whispering Pines*, p. 73.

50   collector: Miss Sears bought two heavily embroidered priests' vestments in Liverpool and was partial to rich red church hangings. In the living room of the home she built later and called the Pergolas she hung a petit point altar piece, from Rouen Cathedral, which depicted Christ walking in a garden and carrying a shepherd's staff. Beneath the tapestry she placed an old English oak choir stall. Though she never visited the Orient, she displayed priestly Chinese robes in cabinets, and her own bed and side table were made from carved Chinese temple screens.

55   "which Bonnat": Museum Archives. Letter from Miss Sears to T. Jefferson Coolidge, Boston Museum of Fine Arts, November 11, 1930.

58   "Our mental attitude": *The Power Within*, for January 1, from Charles B. Newcomb.

      "Tranquillity": Ibid., for November 7, from Katherine Newcomb.

61   "When Clara Endicott Sears decided": Scrap., p. 161, *Boston Transcript*, June 23, 1936.

62   "a villa": Scrap., p. 257, *Worcester Gazette*, June 26, 1961.

      "If a place is to speak": Museum Archives. Letter from Miss Sears to a Miss Bell, October 29, 1939.

Page

Isabella Stewart Gardner: Mrs. Gardner and Fanny Mason traveled to Venice together around 1899, at which time Cousin Fanny bought some eighteenth-century furniture for her new music room at 211 Commonwealth Avenue.

63   "I feel as if": Letters Fruitlands III, p. 16, October 28, probably 1915.

64   "It would have delighted": Letters Fruitlands, p. 2, March 15, 1914.

Chapter 5

65   "When I think": Letters Fruitlands I, p. 11, from the Farm, Danvers, June 19, 1915.

"a necke of land": William C. Endicott, *Memoir of Samuel Endicott* (Boston: by the author, 1924), p. 169. The volume was dedicated to the memory of Clarissa Endicott Peabody.

"told him": Ibid., p. 53

66   "bring his cows": Line-A-Day, December 10, 1927.

"Miss Sears knows exactly": Scrap., p. 56, *Boston American*, March 13, 1932.

67   "If a woman": Scrap., p. 109, *The Press Magazine*, January, 1930.

68   Longfellow: Miss Sears wrote a poem of her own along the same lines and published it in *Wind from the Hills*. The first stanza of "To an Old Empty House" is as follows:

Drear old house,-
Sagged from the weight of years,-
Moss-grown,- neglected,-
How many tears,
Gay peals of laughter,- hopes and fears
In your old face reflected!
We fain would clear our eyes to see
Behind your veil of mystery.

70   "For picturesque beauty": *The Dial*, July, 1843, vol. IV, no. 1, pp. 135-136.

"only through the gates"... "Ordinary secular farming"... "to supersede": Ibid.

Mrs. Alcott: *Bronson Alcott's Fruitlands*, p. 163. Louisa May Alcott wrote an affectionate but unsparing satire on the Fruitlands experiment, "Transcendental Wild Oats." In it, Mrs. Lamb, (Mrs. Alcott) is asked whether there are "any beasts of burden on the place." She answered, "with a face that told its own tale, 'Only one woman!' "

71   "Life was given": *Bronson Alcott's Fruitlands*, pp. 88-89.

"Miss C. E. Sears of this town": Scrap., p. 119, *Harvard Hillside*, August 20, 1932.

72   "though the berries": *Bronson Alcott's Fruitlands*, p. 100.

"Anna and I": Ibid., p. 109.

"I did my lessons": Ibid., p. 111.

73   "was only in the means": Ibid., p. xvi.

NOTES

Page

Alcott's experiment: *The Dial*, April, 1842, vol. II, no. 4, p. 423: The following passage, written by Bronson Alcott in Concord, indicated that he had long been contemplating such a life as was later attempted at Fruitlands. "I planted my seeds and wed my currants and strawberries. I wrought gladly all day, - the air and sun most genial, - and sought my pillow at night with a weariness that made sleep most grateful and refreshing. How dignified and dignifying is labor - and sweet and satisfying. Man, in his garden, recovers his position in the world; he is restored to his Eden, to plant and dress it again. Once more his self-respect is whole and healthful; and all men, apostate though they be, award him a ready and sincere approval."

if a person wanted: *Bronson Alcott's Fruitlands*, p. 105.

Palmer grandson: Scrap., p. 2, *Boston Sunday Herald*, February 15, 1914.

74   "I am glad": Letters Fruitlands I, p. 17.

75   "I am sorry": Letters Fruitlands IV, p. 3, September 10, 1916.

"rendered choice music": Scrap., p. 4, *Clinton Courant*, June 27, 1914. Refreshments were, as always, by William Foster.

Society for the Preservation: Scrap. p. 8, *Clinton Courant*, October 17, 1914.

consommé, quenelles: Receipted bills, Museum Archives. Luncheon for 25 cost $89.38. Linen, utensils, service, two bottles of gin and one of vermouth, plus two pounds of cheese added another $11.17.

76   "As there will be": Scrap. p. 35.

extravaganza at Fenway Court: Cleveland Amory, *The Proper Bostonians* (New York: E. P. Dutton & Co. Inc., 1947), pp. 137-138. At the opening of the Gardner Museum, fifty members of the Boston Symphony performed for an hour, after which guests were treated to the sight of summer gardens flowering in winter within Mrs. Gardner's enclosed courtyard. They then were free to "wander at will through the court, lighted by flame-colored lanterns from the eight surrounding balconies, to the treasure-filled rooms, lit by candles, of the three floors of the [Venetian] palace."

"My chauffeur": Museum Archives.

77   "the view and the surroundings": Museum Archives, June 10, 1930.

"Yesterday was a memorable day": Letters Fruitlands II, p. 11, June 17, no year.

78   "Dear Clara": Letters Fruitlands IV, p. 21, May 9, no year.

"the last sage": Scrap., p. 161. *Boston Transcript*, June 23, 1936. Miss Sears also said he looked very much like Holmes' last leaf on the tree. His biography, *A. Bronson Alcott. His Life and Philosophy*, was published by Roberts Brothers, Boston, 1893.

Sanborn: Letters Fruitlands V, pp. 1, 5, & 6: Mr. Sanborn gave her permission to use his "scattered writings" as she would, asking only that he see proofs before printing. He also read extracts of her work in progress and returned them with "a few slight corrections."

"having devoted herself": Scrap. p. 9, *New York Times*, July 25, 1915.

Page

Scrap. p. 20, June 6, 1915: The *New York Sun* was a bit carried away: "Miss Sears dips her compiler's pen into an ocean of sympathy...."

Scrap., p. 29, *Christian Science Monitor*, September 11, 1915: "Happily Miss Sears allows readers of her compilation to judge for themselves just what Fruitlands was, though she takes care to picture it so that they will respect it as a dignified and well-meant effort on the part of its hero to express his aspirations."

"The story of outward events": Odell Shepard, *Pedlar's Progress* (Boston: Little, Brown and Company, 1937), p. 362.

79　"But I can hardly": Letters Fruitlands III, p. 27, September 5, 1935

newly discovered note: Letters Fruitlands III, p. 26, August 29, 1935. He lists the following items lost in 1844: the Diaries for 1842, 1843, and 1844 to date; "Fruitlands"; Prometheus Papers; Autobiographical Poem; Correspondence for 1840 - 1844 to date; and four books. Shepard goes on to write, "About the year 1850, however, Alcott was again in Albany, and he looked up both the station-master and the railway porter of 1844, making what inquiries he could. Upon his return home he wrote to the New York offices of the railroad and the ferry on which he thought his 'trunk of manuscripts' might have been lost, describing the trunk and its contents in great detail. He never found any clue to the lost articles. But he bewailed the loss again and again in his journals. He reminds himself repeatedly that he must try to make good the loss and fill the gap in his Journals by trying to rewrite the record of these years - the Fruitlands years - from his own recollections, the memories of others, and such papers as he had saved. Of course he never did this - largely, perhaps, because his first few years after the Fruitlands period were filled with physical labor and economic anxieties which left him hardly strength to carry on the Journals for the passing time. But he did do this very significant thing: he had his wife's Journals for the Fruitlands period, badly scrawled though they are and far from sympathetic with the purposes of the enterprise, bound up and numbered so as to serve as a part of his Journal and thus fill the gap as well as circumstances allowed."

"I feel that in publishing": Letters Fruitlands I, p. 18, June 1, 1915.

80　"Take the word": Letters Fruitlands I, p. 55, June 22, 1916.

81　"Then Judge Grant arose": Corporation Records, June 8, 1935.

Chapter 6

82　"The only really successful": *Bronson Alcott's Fruitlands*, p. 45, letter to A. Brooke of Oakland, Ohio, published in *Herald of Freedom*, September 8, 1843.

83　"a farmer going down a country road": Museum Archives. Speech to the Mothercraft Division of the Federation of Women's Clubs, March 3, 1941.

"I well remember": Ibid.

84   "It was impossible"... "Good afternoon"... "Aren't you going"... "Then I began": Museum Archives. Miss Sears' acceptance speech in Cleveland, Ohio, upon receiving an award from the National Society of New England Women, May 18, 1942. The passage is quoted from a rough draft and has been edited for inclusion in this text.

86   "The divine roses": Misc. Letters II, p. 13, December 28, 1904, from Mary Haughton.

"a dear old lady"... "and when you see them": Museum Archives. Miss Sears to Miss Bell, October 29, 1939.

87   "with many tears": Corporation Records, Shaker inventory, 1941.

"They had grown used to me": Museum Archives. Cleveland speech.

"It may be something": Museum Archives. Letter from Olive Heathcote, undated.

88   "endowed with great"... "sought to converse": *Gleanings from Old Shaker Journals*, p. 263.

"From now on": *Bronson Alcott's Fruitlands*, p.121.

"no spontaneous inclination": Ibid., p. 120, letter from Lane to Mr. Oldham.

89   "Lane the transcendentalist": *Gleanings from Old Shaker Journals*, p. 240.

Young William Lane commenced work in the Shoemaker's shop on March 18, 1844, leaving at his father's request, four years later.

"Dearest Auntie": Letters Books I, p. 44.

90   "life was opened"... "a new field": Letters Books V, p. 15, July 15, 1816.

"The Brethren and boys": Museum Archives. Speech, Mothercraft.

91   "beautiful"... "filled them": Ibid.

92   "Six weeks": Museum Archives.

"amid scoffing"... "Men knew": Museum Archives.

"a real factor": Museum Archives.

93   Canning and Evaporating Club: Museum Archives. Details are from a booklet by Miss Sears on the subject.

"Think of the possibility": Scrap., p. 58, *Boston Post*, June 2, 1918.

The Surgeon General's Office approved Pergola Brand soup, though it was never mass produced. When they suggested that she add something to make it less bland, she responded so eagerly that a Harvard Medical School panel pronounced it a bit too savory, but in any case a great improvement over and much more appetizing than the French dried soup known as Maggie Brand. Letters Canning, pp. 16 & 21.

94   "staggering": Letters Canning, p. 20, from Uncle George Peabody, February 11, 1921.

"in a great state"... "At this point": Scrap., p. 52, account of the composition of "Unfurling" from *Living Church*, March 30, 1918.

95   "It is a Baptist song": Scrap., p. 154, *Winthrop Sun and Visitor*, March 16, 1918.

"I know of no one": Misc. Letters I, p. 42, undated.

"Every author is distinct": Museum Archives, July 6, 1921.

At least one other author concurred. Museum Archives. Letter of July 7, 1921, from Henry Beston Sheahan. "I never saw a group photograph of such extraordinary clarity or one more remarkable for good likenesses. The kindly Shakers must have lent their aid to the lens and thinned the air to spirituality."

Chapter 7

97   "When I started writing": Scrap., p. 129, *Worcester Sunday Telegram*, October 26, 1930.

      "to open wide": *The Bell-Ringer*, preface.

98   "Well, Mr. Willis": Museum Archives. Speech to the Harvard Historical Society, June 21, 1938.

      "Before he knew it": Ibid.

101   "toy with love"... "almost dreaded": *The Romance of Fiddler's Green*, p. 50.

      "It's the understanding": *The Bell-Ringer*, p. 267.

      "New England legends": Scrap., p. 64, October 12, 1918.

102   "There was something": Museum Archives. Letter to Mrs. Fraser of Newton, MA, March 13, 1944.

104   "powers lying fallow": *Gleanings from Old Shaker Journals*, pp. 167-168

      Shakers "looked upon life": Museum Archives. Speech, Mothercraft.

      "for yellow": *The Romance of Fiddler's Green*, p. 58.

105   "not that Miss Sears": Scrap., p. 87, *Boston Herald*, March 11, 1922.

      "I am again": Museum Archives.

      "quite in the Hawthorne": Scrap., p. 63, *Boston Transcript*, October, 1918.

106   "The lid was off": Scrap., p. 129, *Worcester Sunday Telegram*, October 26, 1930.

107   "a supply of characteristics": Corporation Records, June 1, 1940.

      "What's she going to do": Scrap., p. 201, *Boston Herald*, December 7, 1941.

      "Please don't write": Misc. Letters II, p. 57.

108   "A family of squirrels": Scrap., p. 178, *Boston Herald*, March 26, 1939.

      "were very nice": Line-A-Day, September 17, 1923.

109   "Dear Miss Clara": Letters Books IV, p. 3, March 16, 1924.

      "was very cordial": Line-A-Day, August 16, 1926.

      "Harvard atmosphere": Letters Books V, p. 49, September 14, 1930.

      Miss Sears' small volume of poems, *Wind from the Hills*, was published in 1936 and included her patriotic poems as well as nature verses. Illustrated with photographs of her garden, the volume was published by G. P. Putnam's Sons after it was turned down by R. N. Linscott of Houghton Mifflin, who wrote, "The note they strike is not rich and deep nor is it intended to be, but for simple, fresh, unpretentious lyrics they seem to me quite admirable...." Museum Archives. August 15, 1935.

Chapter 8

110 "We advised": Young, *Chronicles*, p. 176.

111 *it*... "Am much thinner": Line-A-Day, October 20, 1927.

"Sometimes I think"... "corner-stone": Letters Fruitlands III, p. 11, circa 1927.

112 "careful not to refer": Line-A-Day, July 26, 1925.

"owing to sickness": Line-A-Day, June 9, 1927.

"unquenchable": Line-A-Day, September 24, 1927.

"fired my curiosity": Indian Museum Catalogue, 1941.

113 "strange looking stones": Ibid.

"in her Hooveralls": Scrap., p. 129, *Worcester Sunday Telegram*, October 26, 1930.

"wrote to Mr. West": Line-A-Day, September 19, 1928.

"to be able to hold": Museum Archives. Letter to the Supt. of the Indian Agency, Fort Lapwai, Idaho, 1928.

114 "Now I want": Museum Archives. April 24, 1928.

"no such thing"... "You are dreaming": Museum Archives. February 9, 1929.

115 "get some wonderfully"... "of the utmost importance"... "I realize": Museum Archives. Letter to Col. Welch, November 2, 1928.

"Like yourself": Letters Col. Welch, p. 1, December 30, 1931.

"the aspect of quite": Letters Col. Welch, p. 8, November 7, 1928.

116 "Don't place Sioux leggins": Letters Col. Welch, p. 50, November 18, 1928.

"more for preservation": Letters Col. Welch, p. 17, February 13, 1929.

"out of sympathy": Letters Col. Welch, p. 19, February 28, 1929.

"pretty mean": Line-a-Day, August 18, 1929.

"Mother did not feel": Museum Archives. June 21, 1929.

"had a crash": Line-a-Day, July 1, 1929.

"to state that": Museum Archives. July 19, 1929.

117 "It is useless": Ibid.

"joy of success": Letters Col. Welch, p. 33, July 9, 1929.

"to realize the completion"... "the propriety": Letters Col. Welch, p. 38, January 10, 1930.

"slipping down hill fast": Line-a-Day, August 25, 1929.

"a sort of shock": Line-a-Day, August 26, 1929.

118 "intending to do"... "and slept": Line-a-Day, October 21, 1929.

"tears running": Line-a-Day, October 31, 1929.

"when I think": Misc. Letters III, p. 45, October 10, 1933.

"Her memory will remain": Letters Fruitlands IV, p. 43, from Nixon Waterman, September 7, 1929.

"News came today": Line-A-Day, December 22, 1923.

Page

119 "a splendidly-poised figure": Scrap., p. 117, *Boston Globe*, June 13, 1931.
"would be sent": *The Great Powwow*, p. 23.
"You have shot": Museum Archives.
"a very commanding figure"... account of the unveiling: Corporation Records, June 12, 1931.
120 "Summoning the Lights": Museum Archives.
"a glorious contribution"... "The Indians didn't see"... "looked like royalty": Letters Indians, p. 7, June 13, 1932.
121 "twelve waiters": Corporation Records, July 2, 1938.
"took pains": Ibid.
"symbolized the youthful King Philip": Scrap., p. 170, *Boston Globe*, April 29, 1938.
"did not live to see the day": *The Great Powwow*, p. 100.
122 "in order to show": Ibid.
"profane and dissolute": Young, *Chronicles*, p. 83.
"How the white man": *The Great Powwow*, p. 30.
"easy conditions": Young, *Chronicles*, p. 176.
"avoyde the least scruple": Ibid., p. 159.
"For with all": *The Great Powwow*, p. 26.
123 "the cause was hopeless"... "none the less worthy"... "must be found": *The Great Powwow*, p. 280.
"I got a thrill": Line-A-Day, July 14, 1933.
"throw one wild party": Letters Indians, p. 51, July 18, 1933.
"sound, dependable": Scrap., p. 139, March 18, 1934.
124 "glad to note": Museum Archives.
"great saga": Scrap., p. 138, May 27, 1934.
"never to allow the place": Corporation Records, August 20, 1930.
"Even a policeman": Corporation Records, July 6, 1939.

Chapter 9

Unless otherwise noted, all quotes and anecdotes regarding Miss Sears' research for *Some American Primitives* are from a speech she gave on the subject, a copy of which is in the Museum Archives.
126 "You came...": *Wind from the Hills*.
127 "a man with a very dramatic"... "a way of staring"... "I realized": Corporation Records, July 6, 1939.
130 "as if they were": Scrap., p. 167, *Boston Herald*, February 15, 1938.
131 "real primitives"... "the gradations": *Some American Primitives*, p. vi.
132 "pioneer work": Ibid.
"Doubtless what would please": Scrap., p. 193, *New York Tribune*, January 11, 1942.

NOTES

Page

134   "Everything must be": Museum Archives. Letter of June 20, 1949.

"slim, small": Scrap., p. 226, *Boston Post*, December 15, 1948.

"little corner"... "appalled": The account of the trip is in the Corporation Records, June 27, 1942.

135   "We take unusual pleasure": Museum Archives.

136   "I was very proud": Museum Archives.

"You will be getting ready"... "surrounded"... "Nothing": Museum Archives. April 29, no year.

"courage and fortitude": Museum Archives. Letter from John P. Monks, July 1, 1940.

"a knockout blow": Corporation Records, June 14, 1941.

137   "Sentiment": Ibid.

"atmosphere of peace"... "Being very much curtailed": Corporation Records, June 16, 1945.

"When making the rounds": Corporation Records, June 19, 1943.

138   "exceedingly anxious"... "If I can finish": Corporation Records, June 16, 1945.

139   "1946 has proved itself": Corporation Records, June 15, 1946.

"assembled in a human": Scrap., p. 204, *Savannah Morning News*, February 8, 1948.

"In the good old days": Museum Archives. January 12, 1959.

140   "as a personality": *Savannah Morning News*, February 8, 1948.

"I don't know whether": Scrap., p. 257, *Worcester Gazette*, June 26, 1961.

"I shop"... "for the woman who listens": Scrap., p. 226, *Boston Post*, December 15, 1948.

"bump along"... "when the sprightly": Museum Archives. Letter of September 4, 1956.

141   "and those who are left": Museum Archives. March 23, 1951.

"Your friendship": Museum Archives. Robert Loring to CES, March 20, 1951.

"let our old": Museum Archives. Miss Bassett to CES, February 26, 1953.

"I do not mean to slump": Museum Archives. July 15, 1954.

"I cannot tell you": Museum Archives. April 4, 1954.

"My writing career": Museum Archives. December 11, 1957.

142   "Father continues to improve": Museum Archives. 1957.

"I think only of you": Museum Archives. December 27, 1956.

"cockle shell": Museum Archives.

"All through our growing up": Early Pers. Rem., p. 8.

143   "People say": Scrap., p. 226, *Boston Post*, December 15, 1948.

"We decided": *Early Pers. Rem.*, pp. 11-13.

144   "glad that you have her": Museum Archives. September 4, 1956.

"exactly as I would have ordered it": Scrap., p. 257, *Worcester Sunday Telegram*, March 27, 1960.

"Clara Endicott Sears seems": Scrap., p. 179, *New York Sun*, December, 1941.

Acknowledgments

I would like to thank Richard S. Reed, Director, and the entire Fruitlands staff for their unfailing interest and assistance as I went about my research for this book. I am grateful for the help given me by Fruitlands' former director, the late William Henry Harrison; and I owe a particular debt of gratitude to Pamela Smith for her close reading of the early draft, for her constructive comments, and for her continuing encouragement.

Cynthia H. Barton
Harvard, Massachusetts
October, 1988

INDEX

INDEX

Two thousand copies of this first edition of *History's Daughter* were offset-lithographed from pages prepared by David K. Barton on an IBM Personal System/2®, Model 60, using the Lotus Manuscript® word processing program, and printed on an Apple LaserWriter Plus® in 10-point ITC Bookman type (® International Typeface Corporation). Jacket design and layout by James Rue Design, Harvard, Massachusetts.